*Liturgy
and
Personality*

Dietrich von
Hildebrand

Liturgy and Personality

Foreword by
Alice von Hildebrand, Ph.D.

SOPHIA INSTITUTE PRESS
Manchester, New Hampshire

Liturgy and Personality was first published in 1933 in German. Longmans, Green, and Co. published the first English edition in 1943. A revised English edition was published by Helicon Press, Inc. in 1960. This slightly edited new edition of the 1960 work is published by Sophia Institute with permission of Alice von Hildebrand.

© 1943 Dietrich von Hildebrand; Copyright 1960 Helicon Press, Inc.; 1986 Alice von Hildebrand

Printed in the United States of America

Cover design by Susan Barger

Nihil obstat
  Edward A. Cerny, S.S., D.D.
  Censor Librorum

Imprimatur
  †Francis P. Keough, D.D.
  Archbishop of Baltimore
  March 10, 1960

"The nihil obstat and the imprimatur are official declarations that a book or pamphlet is free of doctrinal or moral error. No implication is contained therein that those who have granted the nihil obstat and imprimatur agree with the content, opinions, or statements expressed."

Library of Congress Cataloging-in-Publication Data

Von Hildebrand, Dietrich, 1889-1977
Liturgy and personality.

Translation of: Liturgie und Persönlichkeit
Reprint. Originally published: Baltimore:
    Helicon Press, 1960.
1. Catholic Church—Liturgy.   2. Personality.
    I. Title.
BX1970.V6513 1985   264'.02   85-18388
    ISBN 0-918477-03-4
    ISBN 0-918477-04-2 (pbk.)

Contents

Foreword

by Alice von Hildebrand
Professor Emeritus
Hunter College

The title *Liturgy and Personality* may puzzle readers. Can a relation exist between these disparate realities —between "liturgy" and "personality"? And yet in this book, Dietrich von Hildebrand succeeds in showing how the Liturgy (when it is approached with the proper attitude and prayed reverently) brings about a profound and rich development, transforming even a modest personality into a great one.

By "great personality," von Hildebrand does not mean one which is magnetic, self-assertive, or able to dominate others through sheer strength of temperament. Rather he understands "great" in its classical sense as indicating *grandeur*: the opposite of mediocrity. The tepidity, indolence, and self-centeredness of the mediocre personality constitute an absolute antithesis to the spiritual alertness, self-giving generosity, and loving abandonment characteristic of a great personality.

Liturgy and Personality

The great personality discerns clearly that which is truly good and that which is not. In his encounters with life, he gives the response that is due to each thing, loving the lovable and abhorring the despicable.

As a result, his actions and attitudes are not governed by merely subjective moods and feelings, but are appropriate responses to persons, things or situations. In this way, he is freed from the metaphysical arrogance and superciliousness typical of those who never grow out of puberty. He breaks the narrow barriers of selfishness and lives in generous communion with others, in friendship and love.

The more such a person succeeds in transcending himself, the richer he becomes: the clearer his mind, the firmer his will, the warmer his heart, the more luminous his consciousness.

Liturgy forms personality

In *Liturgy and Personality*, von Hildebrand reveals the exceptional power of the Liturgy for the forming of such a personality. He shows that the Liturgy embodies in its language and gestures those attitudes toward God, man, and the world which constitute the very core of a truly great personality. The man who lives fully the Liturgy necessarily embraces these attitudes, and develops according to the Divine Model, Christ.

For example, when approaching God through the Liturgy, our attitude should be one of reverence, of alertness, of response-to-value. To the glory of God we are called to respond with praise: "We praise Thee for Thy great glory." In His presence, we are called to acknowledge our sinfulness: "Lord, I am not worthy. . . ." Other prayers in the Liturgy teach us the nature of true communion. We say "*our* Father," not "*my* Father." In such ways, the Liturgy reveals for us the deep bond which exists between all the faithful, opening our eyes to true charity.

When properly understood and lived in an attitude of generous self-giving, the Liturgy teaches us holy discretion. It helps us to grow more recollected. It transforms our mechanistic or purely artificial personal relations into deeply organic ones: with God, our neighbors, and the world.

In *Liturgy and Personality,* Dietrich von Hildebrand discusses many other ways in which the man living in conformity with the Liturgy and vibrating to its spiritual rhythm necessarily undergoes a profound transformation and elevation.

The Liturgy and self-fulfillment

Although in *Liturgy and Personality* von Hildebrand never uses the term "self-fulfillment," the book's theme sheds light on this fashionable concern. It shows that self-fulfillment is not something toward which one should strive but can only be attained *indirectly* as a consequence of striving for a worthy goal. For (as von Hildebrand emphasizes repeatedly) the Liturgy develops personality only when our attention is focused on God and on the proper worship of Him through the Liturgy. As soon as our attention turns away from God and toward ourselves, that development ceases.

Ironically, today's society generally measures the worthiness of a goal in terms of the self-fulfillment it promises. This inversion of the standard has led husbands to leave wives, mothers to leave children, nuns and priests to leave religious life, and thousands of others to strike out in search of self-fulfillment instead of seeking the service and due-response that alone is the path to it. Because these persons have adopted a subjective standard (*self*-fulfillment), they have turned away from the objective world of values. They find themselves spiritually impoverished and starving in a desert of their own choosing.

The power of formal liturgical prayer

In contrast, *Liturgy and Personality* illuminates the role that liturgical worship plays in the development of personality. It teaches us *how* to pray with the Church through the Liturgy: primarily in the Holy Sacrifice of the Mass, but also through the Sacraments, the Sacramentals, and the Divine Office.

Especially today, this is an important topic. For although many people still have a sense for spontaneous, individual prayer, few retain a deep understanding of specifically liturgical worship. Indeed, formal worship and the repetition of standard prayers is often scorned or rejected as hollow and empty worship.

Few know how to approach the sacred mysteries in the Liturgy; few know how to attend Mass and receive the Sacraments properly; few know how to benefit from the treasures the Liturgy contains.

If through the help of *Liturgy and Personality* a person manages to duplicate in his personal life the attitudes which are taught by the Liturgy (attitudes which, when lived, open further the secrets of the Liturgy), he will reach self-fulfillment, even though this will only come as a reward rather than as something directly sought or earned: ''Seek ye first the kingdom of God and His justice, and all the rest will be added to you.''

The perennial essence of the Liturgy

Liturgy and Personality was first published in 1933 in German, translated and published in English in the spring of 1943, revised and reprinted in English in 1960, and is now published in English for the third time. The fact that *Liturgy and Personality* is based on the so-called Tridentine Liturgy which was (up until a short time ago) the official Liturgy of the Roman Catholic Church, in no way detracts from the value of this book today.

The subject of *Liturgy and Personality* is not limited to any particular liturgy; it considers the *essence* of the Liturgy and its relation to the human person. It unveils truths about the Liturgy which are so timeless and so profound that they apply to any official liturgy and help us to understand and participate better in any Divine

Service which the Church offers to the faithful. For as soon as we approach the Altar of God, we are called upon to adopt the attitudes so eloquently described in this book: reverence, awakenedness, and the attitude of response-to-value.

In focusing on the *essence* of the Liturgy in its relation to the formation of personality, *Liturgy and Personality* is truly universal. But this does not mean that there should be only one liturgy or that all liturgies are equally perfect in their glorification of God. The Church in her wisdom has always allowed a pluralism of liturgies. Even today, there are very many. (In the Eastern Church alone, there are currently twenty-one.)

But all liturgies share one central feature: they must aim at glorifying God. In all of them we should adopt the same attitude of reverent adoration. We should participate in the glorification of God insofar as we embrace the spirit of any liturgy. (This fact suggests a standard that ought to guide all liturgists: their work should be such that the Liturgy *properly* glorifies God and draws man into the attitudes appropriate to the worship of God.)

A classic which has received universal praise

Liturgy and Personality reveals *eternal verities* about the Liturgy which are gloriously independent of time or place: truths not derived from empirical facts which are subject to change. For this reason, *Liturgy and*

Personality is not a fashion-item made irrelevant by the passage of time. Nor is it linked to a particular trend in the Church. It is classic in the full sense of the term: perennially true, accessible and enlightening to sincere men of all ages and religious persuasions.

Testimony to the transcendent value and universal appeal of *Liturgy and Personality* is found in the fact that for decades it has been praised by a wide spectrum of people: Church authorities, priests, and lay people (old and young). It is also included in the prestigious Magill's *Masterpieces of Catholic Literature.*

Liturgy and Personality has earned widespread approval because its message has a ring of universal truth and beauty. Moreover, its relevance is not limited to the religious sphere. Its points about value and the response called for by value apply as well to the non-religious side of man's existence. Happy is the man who is discrete, spiritually awake, and who has developed a response-to-value attitude.

A personal testimony

I cannot conclude without mentioning one final point about this book and its source in the soul and life of Dietrich von Hildebrand.

Beyond being a classic on the Liturgy, this book is a very personal testimony about the author's own spiritual life. He fed his soul on the Liturgy, not only by assisting daily at the Holy Sacrifice of the Mass, but also by reciting Vespers and Compline, and this long before he became a Benedictine Oblate.

This is why von Hildebrand was able to write this spiritual gem in only twenty-three days! As he says in his *Memoirs*, ''the fruit was ripe; all I needed to do was to pluck it from the tree.''

The spirit of the Liturgy—and particularly the spirit of response-to-value—was so much the essence of his spiritual and philosophical life that not long before his death he told me: ''If you notice that I am no longer capable of giving the proper response, please call a priest. The end is near.''

A few days before his death, his blood pressure dropped dramatically and he lost consciousness. When he came back to himself, surrounded by a priest and his closest friends, he whispered that he wanted to pray a *Te Deum*, to thank God for all the graces He had given him. Once again (and through the Liturgy), Dietrich von Hildebrand was giving the right response to value.

Conclusion

It is my hope that the reprinting of *Liturgy and Personality* will enable many souls longing for spiritual food to discover the treasures contained in the Liturgy and to feed themselves on this sublime nectar which has been the food of saints through the centuries.

Men are growing increasingly conscious that the wounded and despairing human soul can only find peace in things that transcend the fluctuations of time and fashion. May they discover in *Liturgy and Personality* the message of the Liturgy and duplicate it in their lives. May they learn to find themselves in giving themselves; and may this book help them to do so.

*Liturgy
and
Personality*

Author's Introduction

Liturgy and personality—that is, the spirit embodied in the Liturgy, the spiritual molding of the man who lives in that spirit, and the personality thereby acquired—is one of the widest of themes; for it is the spirit of the God-man that speaks to us in the Liturgy, and a full study of this theme includes both the development of personality and an analysis of the essence both of the Liturgy and of personality. The present work will not attempt to treat this theme in its entirety. Only some of its basic aspects will be considered here, and especially those aspects which more easily escape our attention. In some cases where they are obvious or have been dealt with adequately elsewhere, even very important features will be left to one side. These considerations may help the individual to participate in the celebration of the Liturgy with a deeper awareness, a keener insight into its inexhaustible depths, its classicism, its profoundly organic nature, and a new open-mindedness to its essential pre-eminence over all other forms of devotion. To nothing more than to the Liturgy may that word of Jesus be applied which He cried out to the woman of Samaria: ''If thou didst know the gift of God!''

What is meant by liturgy?

Opinions are divided as to the extent of the meaning of the word ''liturgy.'' Some apply it to all the divine services performed by a priest in the service of the Church, including May Devotions, the Stations of the Cross and other special services, as well as to the holy Mass and the recitation of the Divine Office. Others restrict its scope, as we shall restrict it in this study, to the holy Mass (which is Liturgy in the highest sense), to the Divine Office, and to the administration of the sacraments and sacramentals.

The purpose of this book

Although the present book seeks to stress the exceptional power of the Liturgy for the forming of personality, we must at the same time emphasize that this formation is not the primary intention of the Liturgy.

Author's Introduction

The Divine Office is recited primarily because all praise and glorification is due to God, the fullness of all holiness and majesty, and not because it will bring about a transformation in ourselves. The Liturgy is not primarily intended as a means of sanctification or an ascetic exercise. Its primary intention is to praise and glorify God, to respond fittingly to Him. This intention is expressed in the words of the Gloria in the holy Mass: "We praise Thee, we bless Thee, we adore Thee, we glorify Thee. We give Thee thanks for Thy great glory. . . . For Thou only art holy. . . . Thou only art most high. . . ." The same intention is expressed in the prayer beginning "To the most holy and undivided Trinity (*Sacrosanctae et individuae Trinitati*)" formerly recited at the end of the Divine Office of the day.

The second intention is to ask for the grace of God, but even here the recitation of the Office must not be conceived of as a psychological means of preparing the way for grace, as in the case of fasting, silence, discipline and other such practices considered in a purely ascetic sense. The intention of the Breviary is not to improve our moral life by our own power, but to implore God to grant our religious petitions. Both these intentions are discernible in the Aperi, which preceded the recitation of the Office: "That I may pray this Office worthily, attentively and devoutly, and that I may deserve to be heard in the presence of Thy divine majesty (*Ut digne, attente ac devote hoc officium recitare valeam, et exaudiri merear ante conspectum divinae majestatis tuae*)." The primacy of the first intention of the Office, that of giving fitting praise to God, is distinctly expressed in the concluding words of the prayer: "O Lord, in union with that divine intention with which Thou, whilst on earth, didst Thyself praise God, I offer to Thee these Hours (*Domine, in unione illius divinae intentionis, qua ipse in terris laudes Deo persolvisti, has tibi horas persolvo*)."

To glorify God is also the primary intention of the holy Mass. To this should be added the bestowal of redeeming grace upon men. But holy Mass must never be offered with the sole intent of participating in its graces. The intention of adoring God and sacrificing to Him "through Christ, with Christ and in Christ," is the true condition for renewed incorporation in Christ and the increase of grace.

Finally, as to the sacraments, their primary purpose is man's participation in divine life. In the reception of the sacraments the dominant intention is obviously sanctification and union with God, although, in turn, the final aim of sanctification must be the glorification of God. It is important to grasp that here too, as in the case of holy Mass and the recitation of the Divine Office, to conceive of the sacraments as a psychological means for sanctification—as, for instance, ascetical exercises in themselves—would imply a radical failure to understand their true nature. Although a certain disposition of the person is necessary for the fruitful unfolding of the spiritual life, from the "I do (*volo*)" of Baptism to the contrition required for a true, and even valid, confession, the effect nevertheless cannot be achieved through this disposition as such, but only through a gratuitous act of God, for which man's disposition is only a precondition.

Again, we must particularly stress that in examining the process of personal transformation brought about through the spirit incarnated in the Liturgy, we are not interpreting the Liturgy as some kind of pedagogical means.

To show that such a process of transformation exists does not mean that this is the essential aim of the Liturgy, or that it is the intention with which it is, or should be, carried out. On the contrary, we shall see that one of the special reasons for the strength and depth of the transformation of a personality brought about by the Liturgy is that this transformation is not the end in view; and more than this, that the Liturgy is carried out with another intention entirely. For the deepest transformation of personality occurs, not when means for this transformation are deliberately sought, but when it is brought about in an entirely gratuitous manner through an attitude meaningful in itself. This attitude is like that of love which is entirely directed toward its object, a love which in its very essence is a pure response-to-value, which comes into existence only as a response to the value of the beloved, and which would cease to exist as soon as it became a pedagogical means for one's own improvement. From such an attitude emanates a liberating, mellowing, value-disclosing action of incomparable strength and intensity. And if Plato is right in saying that the soul grows wings as it beholds values, this act of beholding must be understood as an irradiation of the self by the Sun of Values, as a readiness to give oneself to, and to be immersed in, this radiation.The soul grows wings—that is, the deepest inner transformation takes place—only if there is a real penetration of values and a real self-forgetfulness is achieved. Were this act of "beholding values" to become a means of attaining such transformation, at that very moment it would cease to be a genuine irradiation by values, and they no longer would be taken in their proper seriousness; there would no longer be a true communion with the world of values, and the deep transformation would thus be halted.

The deepest *pedagogical* effect is achieved through that which is not used as a *pedagogical means*: It is achieved through that which, independent of pedagogical action, dispenses it as a *superfluum* or gift of superabundance. Thus the deepest and most organic transformation of man in the spirit of Christ is found precisely at that point where we purely respond to values, in the giving up of ourselves to God's glory, in the glorifying of God performed as divine service, in the abiding *Coram ipso* (in standing before Him), in the rejoicing in God's existence, in the *Gloria Domini* (the glory of the Lord), in the *magnalia Dei* (the great deeds of the Lord). As we pray and sacrifice liturgically—and this means through Christ, with Christ and in Christ—glorifying God, we "put on Christ" (*induere Christum*) as the Liturgy boldly expresses it.

But need we stress this action and invest it with a conscious meaning, since it comes about of itself, and, even more, must not be aimed at for itself? Yes, for in the first place, in disclosing the fundamental attitudes embodied in the Liturgy, we come to a deeper understanding of the Liturgy and its spirit, which enables us to perform it more consciously and genuinely. And more than this, the Face of Christ is revealed in the Liturgy: the Liturgy is Christ praying. To learn the fundamental dispositions embodied in the Liturgy means to penetrate more deeply into the great mystery of the adoration of God, which is Jesus Christ. The more consciously the spirit of Christ is grasped and lived in the Liturgy, and the more the Liturgy becomes for us an "imitation of Christ," the deeper the transformation of man in Christ.

Moreover, today we are in urgent need of such a study, for there are many who still prefer other forms of devotion and religious exercises. They do not recognize the fact that it is precisely in the Liturgy that there are presented to us, in the deepest and most organic form, the fruits of the divine life received by us in baptism, and that the man who is entirely formed by the spirit of the Liturgy is most like unto Christ. Not that this formation can be achieved only through the Liturgy! God is able to raise up out of stones children of Abraham. He may give this spirit to a man who has but scant familiarity with the Liturgy and prays little according to the forms of the Liturgy. But in each saint, in whom the image of Christ shines anew, the spirit of the Liturgy lives. Perhaps it cannot always be found in his teachings or in the forms of devotion introduced by him, but it is there in his sanctity, in the fact of his being a saint. It still remains true that the

Liturgy and Personality

Liturgy, in its organic relation to inner prayer and asceticism is the God-given path for growth in Christ. Toward those for whom this fact is still hidden, our hearts must always echo with the words already quoted: "If thou didst know the gift of God!"

I

The Liturgy
and the Vocation of Man

The meaning of all creation is the imitation and glorification of God, the inconceivably glorious and holy One. That which is created—whether it belongs to the domain of pure matter (as the sea or the mountains) or to the realm of organic life (as the plant and animal) or to the sphere of spiritual things (as a work of art, a cultural epoch, a community, or the spiritual person himself)—exists only in order to imitate and glorify God, in fulfilling the divine idea in its regard, and simultaneously bringing to fruition the fullness of values to which it is ordained. For all values— goodness, beauty, the mystery of life, the noble light of truth, and even the dignity of being itself (as opposed to nothingness)—all these are rays which radiate from God's being, Who is all holiness. Whatever is good and beautiful, all that possesses a value, is a reflection of His eternal light and imitates God according to its own fashion.

Values are not only like a dew falling from heaven, but also like incense rising to God; each value, in itself, addresses to God a specific word of glorification. A being, in praising God, praises Him through its value, through that inner preciousness which marks it as having been drawn out of the indifferent. Nature praises God in its beauty not only by speaking of God to man and inspiring him to praise God, but also by the silent praise rising from its own beauty. This is true of every work of art, every perfect community, every truth, every moral attitude. Man, the most precious creature known to us through experience (who is not only a trace [*vestigium*] of God, but also an image [*imago*] of God), is called not only through his value to be objective praise of God, like all the rest of creation, but also to a consciously-accomplished glorification.

Man alone can make a conscious response to God's endless glory. He must first of all respond adequately to each value as a reflection of God; he must respond with joy, enthusiasm, veneration, love; and above all he must adoringly love and lovingly adore God, Who is the fullness of all value. For this glorification of God, voiced in loving adoration, represents quite a new dimension of glorification, a different degree of reality, as new as the personal being of the subject, this awakened being, penetrated with lucid consciousness—in radical distinction to all impersonal being. The ultimate dignity of man consists precisely in that he can consciously adore and glorify God. But this conscious response to God's glory, which belongs to the ultimate significance of man, does not stand juxtaposed to his vocation to praise God through his own value (and ultimately through his saintliness), but is closely linked with it. In man, the central personal values do not take shape ''on their own'' as does his physical stature or his temperament; they grow, on the contrary, out of man's experienced communion with the world of values, out of his conscious turning to the realm of values, out of his act of giving himself up to God through his affirmation of values and his response to them. A person can never be good, if he does not will the good, rejoice in it and love it. He cannot attain sanctification without adoring God, without loving Christ and bending his knee before Him.

Thus, the illumination received from the world of values and from the Face of Christ, and the conscious response to God's glory, are the conditions for man's inner transformation, the ripening of the central personal values, and, above all, of the supernatural beauty by which God is objectively praised and glorified. Conversely this ''word'' of praise is the more adequate and authentic, according to the degree that a man is more perfect. The vocation to adore God and to glorify Him through conscious acts can be fulfilled by man only to a degree that all the central values are realized in him, and, above all, to the degree that he resembles Christ, that is to say, is saintly. Thus, the two currents of praise and glorification—the objective silent one, expressed through values, and the personally-performed, conscious adoration—must not be divided in man. They mutually condition each other, and the growth of the one means the increase of the other.

The conscious glorification of God is, however, also twofold in character. Not only do we owe God adoring love expressed, on the one hand, in the affirmation of all values and, on the other, in the immediate love of God; we also owe Him *spoken* praise, an uttered act of glorification. Inasmuch as we are spiritual persons, we are capable of a clearly-formulated praise, of referring ourselves expressly to glorification, of an uttered "word" of praise. This uttered praise is organically linked to adoring love, but it brings something new in relation to the latter. According to the words of St. Augustine this expressed glorification will also resound in eternity: "We shall repose and we shall see, we shall see and we shall love, we shall love and we shall praise, and so it will be at the end without end (*Vacabimus et videbimus, videbimus et amabimus, amabimus et laudabimus, quod erit in fine sine fine*)."

The praise of God (*laudare*), in which we join in the "Sanctus" of the angels, is something other than the love of God (*amare*). To be sure, it flows forth out of adoring love, for the *amare* is the very soul of praise; but the expressed act of praise, lauding and glorifying, responds in yet another way to the glory of God. It is an extension of the act of adoring love, a confirmation of it, and a seal upon it. While the specific glorification of God is contained more implicitly in adoring love (and adoring love is more like an ultimate and suitable response to God's endless glory and holiness), the act of praising, lauding and thanksgiving is an expressed gesture of glorification, a personal realization of that very glorification which is objectively conveyed through values.

This expressed glorification of God is also correlated with the objective glorifying of God through saintliness. The saint alone is capable of *authentically* praising God. As the Twenty-third Psalm puts it: ''Who shall ascend into the mountain of the Lord or who shall stand in His holy place? The innocent in hands and clean of heart.'' But then, it is through expressed glorification and praise (which finds its supreme expression in the holy Sacrifice of the Mass), that man is deeply transformed and sanctified. These two forms of glorification cannot therefore be separated. Of course, there still exists a certain order of succession, as expressed in the words of St. Augustine already quoted. Sanctification and adoring love go hand in hand, and the specific *laudare* and *glorificare* are organically linked to them both. ''*Cantare amantis est* (To sing is the act of the lover),'' St. Augustine also says. But this order of succession in spiritual formation does not mean that these forms of divine glorification actually follow such a sequence in time.

We shall better grasp the truth that the sanctification of man is entirely impossible without the *laudare* and *glorificare Dominum*, after the following basic fact is examined:

Only the God-man, Jesus Christ, can truly offer adoration and love to God. He alone is entirely holy, He alone truly glorifies God through His holiness, and He alone can truly praise God. The final, supernatural

vocation of every man is, therefore, transformation into Christ. Only from Christ, with Him, and in Him,
can we offer true adoring love to God and praise Him;
and we can become holy only to the extent that we
cease to live, and Christ lives in us; that is to say, to the
extent that the divine life implanted in us in baptism is
fully developed. Our transformation into Christ is the
essence of sanctity. This transformation of man into
Christ includes not only the loving adoration of the
Father with Christ and in Christ, but also the participation in the sacrifice of Christ and in the uttering of the
"word," the only true praise and glorification, addressed by Christ to His heavenly Father. Even now,
in spite of our imperfection and infirmity, we are per-
mitted to join in the praise of the angels, because as
members of the Mystical Body of Christ, we pray *with*
the Head. And the more fully we participate in this expressed glorification of the Father in the *laudare*, the
more we shall be transformed into Christ. We are
drawn increasingly into the adoring love of Christ for
the Father in that very action by which we consciously
present to the Father the fruit of that adoring
love—that is, the *laudare* and *glorificare*.

Of course, this alone does not suffice for the full
transformation into Christ. Apart from the indispensable foundations (participation in divine life through
baptism, and its renewal and confirmation through the
sacraments), there is the loving immersion in Christ,
living and acting according to the spirit of Christ,
following His teaching, following Christ by carry-
ing His cross, loving one's neighbor with Christ. All

ascetic practices, all the "daily work" involved in our striving for perfection, serve only this one purpose. But one of the basic factors leading to transformation into Christ is participation in His uttered glorification of the Father, and this glorification takes place especially in the Liturgy. It leads us into the secrets of the love of the God-man for the Father and His glorification of the heavenly Father, and the love of the heavenly Father for man. The conscious, fully-awakened act of performing the Liturgy imprints upon the soul the Face of Christ. In taking part in the Liturgy, we make our own the fundamental attitudes embodied in it.

It is with this process of transformation that the present book deals. Herein will be expounded the imitation of Christ which is organically achieved through participation in the Liturgy, though it should be remembered that the Liturgy is not performed for that express purpose. We have previously described the three specific vocations of man: the silent praise of God through the possession of the Christian virtues, the adoring love of God, and the expressed *laudare* and *glorificare*. This book concerns itself with the formative power of the last for the first two, that is, with the formative power of the *laudare* and *glorificare* with Christ and through Christ. But, as we have already said, only a part of this theme will be dealt with here. We shall not speak of the relation of the spirit embodied in the Liturgy to sanctity as a whole, but only of certain elements of sanctification, which are less familiar to us, because they are not

Liturgy and Personality

explicitly mentioned in the Commandments of God and in the demands emphasized by Catholic ethics. The most important and central elements will be intentionally excluded, such as, for instance, how man, formed by the spirit of the Liturgy, grows into the love of Christ, and so on.

We shall especially consider here the formative power of the Liturgy on the very structure of the personality, on these elements which, though indispensable as a basis for sanctification, are not its central point, with which the Sermon on the Mount deals. This restriction is made in order not to repeat what has already been said. But this restriction, which obliges us to limit ourselves to the personality-forming power, in the narrower sense of the word, has nothing whatever to do with the aesthetic overrating of that which is commonly called "personality." We are as far removed as possible from the "cult of personality" which places above the simple fact of humbly obeying God's Commandments the question of whether or not a man is a full "personality." "Only one thing is necessary": the glorification of the Father through the imitation of Christ and participation in His glorification. This however implies being a personality in its true sense; that is, the saint alone is the true and complete man, and the true personality. Thus our present study forms but a part of that other great theme: "Be you therefore perfect, as also your heavenly Father is perfect."

II

The Essence of Personality

In speaking of personality as distinct from the person, we have in mind something clearly defined. Every man is a person in that his being is essentially conscious; and he is a subject who enters into relations with others, who knows, wills, and loves. A person is a being who "possesses himself," who does not simply exist but who actively achieves his being, and has the power to choose freely. But every man is not a personality. Only persons can be personalities, but in order to be a personality it is not enough just to be a person.

When then is a man a personality?

The average man, the inoffensive, colorless, ordinary man without a clearly expressed individuality is not a personality. But neither is the abnormal man, the crank who astonishes others because of his peculiarities and falls out of the common range because of his oddities and eccentricities. Nor can the pathological man be considered a personality. A personality in the true sense of the word is the man who rises above the average only because he fully realizes the *classical human* attitudes, because he knows more deeply and originally than the average man, loves more profoundly and authentically, wills more clearly and correctly than the others, makes full use of his freedom; in a word—the complete, profound, true man.

To confuse the "normal" man and the "average" man is an error typical of the narrow-minded Philistine. This error holds that the ordinary, average, run-of-the-mill type is the normal man, and that the one who differs from the average is the abnormal man, regardless of whether he is above or below the average—or simply "outside" it. The genius and the insane man are seen as related because both of them stand outside the range of the average man. But statistics do not decide what the normal man is. The most numerous type is not necessarily the normal. The normal is that which most closely corresponds to the essence of man. That man is a personality who most fully develops this essence, who realizes entirely all the essential personal values. "Personality" is a mark of the normal man because in him the specifically personal is most fully and originally developed. The average man is not the normal man; he is a spiritually immature and crippled man. Indeed, the full personality, who surpasses the average, is so little akin to the abnormal or psychopathic that we have rather to say that the average man—the common type in whom the classical human attitudes are not fully expressed and freely developed—is the one who, more often than not, in one respect or another, manifests abnormal traits: inhibitions, infantilisms, repressions.

Neither, of course, should the normal man be confused with the man who possesses all gifts and talents. The truly normal is the classical man who is fully perceptive of values and responsive to them, the uncramped objective man, liberated from the prison of himself, in whom the capacity for self-donation and love is unbroken. These truly normal men are those who are filled with so deep a thirst for happiness that harmless little joys cannot satisfy them, who stand in a direct elementary relation to all things, not rendered insipid and commonplace by conventions: men like St. Augustine and St. Francis, even before their conversions. On the other hand, special gifts, philosophic and artistic genius for instance, gifts such as those possessed by Michelangelo, Beethoven, Goethe, are gifts of God which do not belong to the normal man, as such, in the strict sense of the word. They are *exceptional* gifts, not only because they are rare—normal men are also—but because they represent special powers which are *not indispensable to man's essence*, or to his general vocation; they are extraordinary values and gifts which only certain men receive from God. Every normal man, in our sense of the word, is a personality, but this does not mean that he is a genius. Under the term "personality" we understand the complete, classical man, in whom are revealed the great fundamental traits of man, undistorted, and unbroken.

Two main components of personality must here be distinguished: in the first place, the fullness of the essential spiritual "organ," the faculty of loving and knowing, the power of will, the natural potential of the person, the intensity of life which flows in him—we might say his "essential endowment," as distinct from special talents; in the second place, the organic link with the world of values and of truth, the perception of them, the response to them, the living in truth, in tune with the objective logos, and the absence of all subjective deviations from the meaning of being. Neither of these two elements, taken separately, is sufficient for the constitution of personality. The first is a pure gift which we receive and to which we can add nothing, just as we cannot add a cubit to our physical stature. The second is, on the contrary, under the sway of our freedom.

Usually, the question whether or not a man is a personality is inadequately concerned only with the presence of the first element. In the cult of personality inspired by a Napoleon, a Goethe and many others, we are so carried away by the scale of this component that we do not notice those points which reveal a certain emptiness and lack of substance, a limitation and "impotence": those points where these men deviate from the objective logos, and thus do not draw life from the genuine world of God. On the other hand, it is true that a man who has received a humble and limited "essential endowment" may, by the best intentions and by service and sacrifice to the world of values, cease to be an average man, though he does not possess the usual scope, power and fullness of true personality. For the formation of personality both components must exist, not only side by side, but organically linked together.

A further distinctive trait of personality is that the entire being possesses unity of *style*. Its external being is not inorganically and outwardly stamped on the inner being, but is a genuine projection of the latter. There is a rare harmony between the inner and the outer being in those men whose speech, expression, movements, external style of life are organically molded by their inner attitudes. Such men radiate a noble and powerful atmosphere; they are not dragged down to a lower level by the accidental conditions of their environment.

The power of emanating an atmosphere is not in itself, however, a sign of true personality. A man may also powerfully radiate a vulgar, trivial, common, and vain atmosphere. In such a case, he is not a personality in the true sense of a word that designates a genuine and exalted value. The unity of style must be the expression of the true, authentic atmosphere of a life rooted in the metaphysical situation of man, of an attitude open to value and responding to value, and permeated by the supernatural world.

After what has been said, it is not further necessary to try to prove that the word "personality" is used incorrectly and inadequately when it is applied to men who possess a strong character, who assert themselves and occupy a certain "space" because of their temperament. The power of self-assertion, whether expressed in a stream of irresistible vitality, or in strong formal energy and a keen sense of the aim pursued, is not sufficient to achieve personality in the deeper sense of the word. Neither does this alone constitute the individuality of certain persons, especially persons already possessed of those qualities which cause us to define them as leaders: a certain conquering fullness and spiritual energy which makes them central figures, around whom other human beings rally and crystallize, and, so to speak, form a community. Even this power is only a special manifestation of the first component of personality: the full, natural, "essential endowment." Its presence does not in any way guarantee the presence of a second indispensable component; and its lack does not imply a lack of personality. There are quiet personalities, emanating only secret, hidden radiations.

A further question is whether it is possible for every man to become a personality. Are not man's capacity for perceiving values, his unbroken power of responding to them, his fullness and breadth, conditioned by his talents? Are there not insignificant men, stupid, ungifted, limited, who with the best of intentions cannot hope to achieve for themselves the fullness, breadth and freedom which belong to true personality? And what of inwardly insecure, unstable people who let themselves be overthrown by every breath of spiritual wind, brushed aside by the least pressure? What of those who in a new, impressive environment feel the ground slipping from under their feet, who are hopelessly carried away by the stream of public opinion, by the fashionable or sensational? Are they not sheeplike, average men, the very opposite of personalities?

Yes, considered from the purely natural point of view. For a Goethe, for instance, there exist two categories of men: middling men who possess at best a modest "essential endowment," and "*personalities*." According to this, it would be absurd to expect a middling man to become a personality, just as it would be absurd to expect a man not musically gifted to become a Mozart.

But we cannot be content with a purely natural point of view, for everything now bears the mark of the almost inconceivable exaltation of humanity through the Incarnation of God and through the baptism which implants in man a new principle of life, participation in the life of Christ and the Holy Trinity. To the extent that every baptized person develops this life himself, or, more accurately, lets this life be developed in him, to the extent that he gives himself up to Christ and follows Christ, living from Christ, with Christ and in Christ—he lives no more but Christ lives in him: he thus participates in the unlimited breadth and fullness of Christ. He who is immersed in the life of Christ, he in whom Christ is truly imitated, the saint, becomes a personality, no matter what his "essential endowments" are. Of course, grace does not replace but transfigures nature. If an intellectually ungifted man attains sainthood, he does not suddenly acquire a philosophical or theological genius. Among saints, too, we find the same differences as between geniuses and plain, simple, not especially gifted men. But the lack of gifts and the modest natural structure are no longer something depressing, narrowing and limiting, because they have been transformed into that moving simplicity which is penetrated with the supreme wisdom of Jesus Christ; because the question of intellectual "significance" is surpassed through the participation in the unutterable breadth of God, in the pulsations of the Most Sacred Heart, in Whom are all the treasures of wisdom and knowledge, *"in quo sunt omnes thesauri sapientiae et scientiae."*

The saint is strong in his weakness because he has fully developed the supernatural life received in baptism, that is, the new principle of life, new "organs" and powers. The saint, therefore, shows forth always the two components of personality in a far higher sense: the supernatural "essential endowment," and the complete organic link with the world of supernatural values, holiness and the mysterious glory of God which has revealed itself in the Face of Christ. In this response to the supernatural, all ties with the natural world of values are contained *per eminentiam.*

To speak of St. John Vianney, the Curé of Ars, St. Conrad of Parzham, or Bl. Brother Juniper as significant persons—even to raise such a question—is to betray a complete lack of understanding of the world of the supernatural. The person of every saint—and this means one who no longer lives in himself but in whom Christ lives—breathes a fullness, a breadth and height, whose brightness surpasses even all the fullness and greatness of the highest purely-natural genius. The average man, in his petty limitations, is further removed from the world of the most simple saint, with the most modest natural endowment, such as St. John Vianney, than he is from the rich intellectual world of a Goethe. The world of the saint is by far the more classical, universal, illuminating; in it the breath of truth is felt in an incomparably higher degree. This does not mean that saints receive an analogous natural talent through saintliness, but that they receive this light and fullness in Christ *per eminentiam.*

To die in ourselves, in order that Christ may live in us, is thus the only path leading to full personality in a far truer and higher sense of the word; and it is this path which is open through the grace of God even to those who possess only a humble natural "essential endowment." This dying to oneself, does not, however, mean the giving up of individuality. On the contrary, the more a man becomes "another Christ," the more he realizes the original unduplicable thought of God which he embodies. Of course, this is only possible because Christ is the "Son of Man," because the whole of humanity is contained in Him, and above all, because He is not only man, but the "entire fullness of the Godhead lives in His heart (*in quo est omnis plenitudo divinitatis*)." Every imitation of a man, even of the greatest, richest, most gifted man, even of a genius, would mean the giving up of one's individuality, a leveling, a renunciation of personality, not to mention the fact that an absolute, literal imitation of any man is entirely impossible. In relation to Christ, it is quite the opposite. The mysterious truth is that the unique inimitable design of God is fully and ultimately realized in a man only when he is transformed into Christ. Can one find more powerful, more deeply expressed individualities than St. Catherine of Siena, St. Francis of Assisi, St. Augustine, St. Paul, St. Gregory VII?

Nevertheless it should be borne in mind that it would be a great mistake to place before ourselves the specific aim of becoming personalities in this higher sense of the word, or of becoming powerful individuals. High as the value is which inheres in the participation in the breadth and fullness of God, in becoming a true personality, nevertheless, this is not the *unum necessarium*; it is subject, in a most special way, to the word of Jesus: ''Seek ye first the kingdom of God and His justice, and these things shall be added unto you.''

III

Liturgy and Personality

As the preceding chapter has already indicated, a distinction must be made between the two fundamental elements in the formation of personality and its development in general. The first is the purely ontological basis for the development of personal life, which man can in no way bestow upon himself; it is a pure gift from the hand of God, in the giving of which, man's freedom can play no part. This *natural* basis is the existence of man as a spiritual person, the presence of spiritual "organs" such as the powers of knowing, willing, loving. To these should be added the special natural tendencies received by man through heredity. The *supernatural* basis of the imitation of Christ is the divine life implanted by baptism, and which is restored, fortified, or supplemented in us through the other sacraments. In this life, which makes us members of the Mystical Body of Christ and which is not only a moral but a mysterious physical link with Christ—bestowed as a pure gift of God—is found the ontological basis for the transformation into Christ, the vital principle of all saintliness. To be endowed with this supernatural life presupposes the existence of the natural ontological basis, that is to say, the essence of the person. Such a supernatural life could never be granted to an inanimate thing, or to a merely living creature such as a plant or an animal.

The second, no less indispensable and fundamental element of all natural and supernatural formation of personality, is the intentional contact* with the world of values. We have already seen that natural moral values do not arise of themselves, as do, for example, temperament or physical beauty. They can only grow through the apprehension and affirmation of values, through a conscious response to them. The simple faculties of knowing, willing, and loving do not yet imply virtues; these spiritual "organs" do not confer humility, purity, love. Virtues only blossom out of the conscious union of man with the world of values. It is the same in regard to the supernatural life of man. This fundamental element of "intention" in spiritual growth is not excluded from the supernatural realm, and, for adult man, this conscious turning to God is demanded even for membership in the Mystical Body

* [*Ed. note*: Here von Hildebrand employs the technical philosophical sense of the term *intentional*, meaning by *"intentional contact* with values" a *conscious awareness* of them.]

of Christ, as is shown in the *volo* (I do) of the baptismal rite, as well as in the existence of the baptism of desire and the baptism of blood. *"Qui fecit te sine te, non te justificat sine te* (Who made you without you, will not justify you without you),'' says St. Augustine, and what is true of justification is also true of sanctification. Without the knowledge of Christ and of the Father as revealed in the Holy Face, without the love of Christ, the epiphany of the invisible Father, without the following of Christ, no one can be sanctified. "I am the way, and the truth, and the life,'' says the Lord; and, "he who beholdeth me, beholdeth also the Father.''

Without the ultimate free "yes'' of dedication to Christ the God-man, without a total giving of self to Christ, without the taking up of His cross, without the following of the greatest commandment "on which dependeth the whole law and the prophets,'' the divine life implanted in us through baptism cannot reach its full development in us. "If anyone loves me, he will keep my word. And my Father will live in him, and we will come to him, and will make our abode with him.''

The meaning of the Liturgy for the formation of personality will be considered here from the point of view only of the second fundamental element, the *intentional* root of sanctity, and not from the point of view of the ontological influence. This purely ontological basis will be taken for granted, and therefore more stress will be put naturally on holy Mass and the Divine Office than on the sacraments in which the ontological causality stands foremost.

Liturgy and Personality

When we examine the spirit embodied in the Liturgy, which informs itself upon the person who participates in the Liturgy, it appears that this spirit is revealed in three ways.

First of all, the spirit of the Liturgy is expressed in the liturgical act as such, in the holy Sacrifice of the Mass, the eternal loving sacrifice of Christ; in the sacraments, the communicating love of Christ; and in the Divine Office, the loving adoration and eternal praise which Christ offers to His heavenly Father.

In the second place, the spirit of the Liturgy expresses itself in the meaning and atmosphere conveyed by single prayers, antiphons, hymns, and the like, in all that the Liturgy expressly *says*, in the thought and spiritual climate which pervade its forms and words.

In the third place, the spirit of the Liturgy is expressed in its structure and construction: in the architecture of the Mass, of the rites, of the different sacraments, of the Divine Office, in the sucessive accentuation of praise, thanksgiving and prayer, in the structure of the Liturgical Year, in the rules according to which, for example, one feast takes precedence over another.

We shall attempt to examine certain fundamental features of the homogeneous spirit which is expressed in these three sources, and to show that these fundamental features are indispensable to the formation of a true personality.

We are not interested in historical questions regarding the epoch to which this or that part of the Liturgy belongs; what motives inspired their introduction into the Liturgy; whether they are of Roman, Gallican, or Oriental origin. We are interested in the mysterious, all-embracing, qualitatively expressed unity of this spirit of the Church, of Christ Who continues thus to live among us, of the Liturgy as the voice of the Church. For the building of this Church, materials were gathered from the most diverse cultures and epochs; but the unity of which we speak is not thereby broken, even when the reasons which prompted the introduction of this or that element are secondary and fortuitous. Though a historical analysis carried out in its own place and time may prove fruitful and be justified, there is no room for it in our study. We are not interested in the formation of ancient or medieval, Roman or Oriental man, but in the formation of the supernatural personality in us, the formation of Christ in us, as it has taken place in every saint—not in his words and teachings, not in the form of asceticism he has chosen, but in his saintliness—in a St. Augustine as well as a St. Thérèse of the Child Jesus, in a St. Benedict as well as in a St. Francis, in a St. Bernard as well as in a St. Vincent de Paul.

IV

The Spirit of Communion in the Liturgy

One of the deepest marks of the Liturgy is its character of communion-prayer. In the holy Mass and in the Divine Office not only does the *We* dominate the *I*, but even when the *I* is uttered, as in "O God, come to my assistance (*Deus, in adjutorium meum intende*)," or in the Confiteor, or in "Lord, I am not worthy (*Domine, non sum dignus*)," or in the Psalms, this *I* is completely incorporated in the communion. It is uttered as issuing from the ultimate union of all in Christ, which precludes the omission or exception of other members of the Mystical Body. The Liturgy, as the official prayer of the Church, the prayer of the Mystical Christ, is, in its very meaning and essence, the prayer of a community; each man, even when praying alone, enters consciously, if he understands this prayer, into the wider stream of prayer; he takes part in the prayer of the Head and through Him also of the Mystical Body of Christ. This distinguishes the Liturgy from the other forms of prayer and devotion, as for instance the Rosary, the Stations of the Cross, May devotions, or ordinary private prayer. Of course, even these prayers should issue from the spirit of ultimate union with all the members of the Body of Christ, although they do not force us to enter that spirit. As a prayer rising from the ultimate depths, and bearing the most true and classical expression of supernatural reality, liturgical prayer possesses an incomparable communion-forming power. For we must not forget that values possess a unifying power; and the higher the value in question, the greater this power. In beholding a value, in grasp-ing it, the soul of the individual is not only "recollected," drawn out of "distraction," but the barrier isolating him from other men is lifted. Every true value, such as the beauty of nature or of a mas-terpiece of art like Beethoven's *Ninth Symphony*, or the moral light of a generous act of forgiveness, or of an immovable fidelity, all these values which speak to us of God and touch our hearts, draw our spirit toward the true world of God, lead us before the face of God, and, thanks to them, the barriers of pride, egoism and self-assertion that isolate us and make us look upon our fellow men from without as adver-saries and competitors, fall away.

The higher the value, the more we become aware of this ultimate objective unity in God. This fact takes on an entirely new sense when we come to the supernatural world of holiness, and especially when we contemplate Christ, when the glory of Christ, of "the only-begotten of the Father, full of grace and truth," touches our heart. We inwardly achieve this objective union as members of the Mystical Body of Christ to the degree that we become inebriated with Christ. For it is not true that the highest "I-and-thou-communion" with Christ destroys communion with other men, causing us to forget others, to have no more place for them in our hearts. On the contrary, to the extent that we love Jesus, and that a mysterious relationship is formed with Him and we lovingly grow into Him, to the extent that we participate in His love for our neighbor, and the phrase "the love of Christ impels us (*amor Christi urget nos*)," becomes alive in us, we reach that final point of depth where alone the ultimate, personally-achieved communion can be formed; in other words, we truly reach the point where we become aware of the ultimate supernatural unity with all men in Christ. It is a specific error found in liberalism, and also found widely in Protestantism, to believe that the more a thing is peripheral, the more it leads toward the spirit of communion; and that, on the contrary, the more deeply we are moved by something and the higher the value in question, the more we are plunged into solitude. The opposite is true. Those goods isolate which are merely subjectively satisfying. The world of authentic values, on the contrary, unites. And God, the deepest theme of each of us, the highest good, is at the same time the most general theme, of which we cannot be absolutely conscious unless we are also conscious of our ultimate deepest communion with all men.

The atmosphere of the Liturgy is saturated with Christ, with the hidden God revealed in Christ. Not only does it deal with God as do other prayers; more than all else it shows us the ultimate all-embracing entirety of supernatural reality; it speaks from the ultimate truth of the metaphysical situation of man; it reflects God's Face in a unique adequateness; it speaks the language of Christ; it envelops us in an atmosphere of eternity which soars above the limitations of particular times and places. Truly, when we stand in this world of the Liturgy, when we are enfolded by it, we witness the *Phase Domini*, the "Passing of the Lord." In it we touch Christ without any sort of falsification or subjective alteration. It therefore awakens us to that true, ultimate consciousness of communion, that ultimate, victorious union in love which is the very opposite of all human relationships of boisterous good-fellowship. It is the very opposite also of all easy familiarity, of the "smug society spirit" which is nothing else but a falling into the periphery together, and only means isolation in the depths. The Liturgy alone, because of its supraindividual stamp, its all-embracing breadth, never violates man's separate individuality. As for other prayers, it is always possible for them to bear an individual mark and for this reason they cannot be imposed on everybody without an unwarranted pressure. This can be true of the most beautiful prayers of some of the saints, of a St. Gertrude, for instance, to say nothing of certain hymns whose sentimental and trashy nature is a falsification of the spirit of Christ.

This supraindividual character of the Liturgy is at the same time the very opposite of colorless neutrality or of a bloodless stereotype; it combines holy sobriety with the greatest ardor, eternal calm with the deepest emotion, holy fear with holy joy and winged peace; all these are mingled in that *coincidentia oppositorum*, that meeting of opposites, as found only in God Who is the *Sum*, and in Whom all values are contained *per eminentiam*. Each individuality, however strongly expressed, can take part in this supraindividual prayer; and one can take part in it without having to give up or disavow that special secret word that God utters anew to each soul, in that each soul represents a unique, unduplicable design of God.

This mysterious principle inherent in the Liturgy adds to all which it makes its own—the sermon of each saint, each prayer, even the apostles' epistles—a deeper beauty and actuality, something that shines more brightly than these same texts isolated from their liturgical context. Thus, for instance, Jeremias' lamentations in the Tenebrae, or the words of St. Paul in the Epistle of Holy Saturday: ''Brothers, therefore, if you be risen with Christ, seek the things that are above; where Christ is sitting at the right hand of God. Mind the things that are above, not the things that are upon the earth. For you are dead; and

Liturgy and Personality

your life is hid with Christ in God. When Christ shall appear, Who is your life, then you also shall appear with Him in glory.'' With what a new significance, with how much more mysterious an actuality, do these words shine! Thus also the words of St. Leo, St. Gregory and St. Augustine in the Christmas Matins, or in St. Peter's Epistle on Easter Saturday: ''But you are a chosen generation, a kingly priesthood, a holy nation, a purchased people: that you may declare His virtues Who has called you out of darkness into His marvelous light (*Vos autem genus electum, regale sacerdotium, gens sancta, populus acquisitionis: ut virtutes annuntietis ejus, qui de tenebris vos vocavit in admirabile lumen suum*).''

The individuality of each saint and apostle differs, yet the spirit and rhythm of the Liturgy are one. The spirit of them all is inserted into the Liturgy and serves it; while the Liturgy, in turn, brings to light that which is deepest in their words, pervading it with the rhythm of the Liturgical Year. The very words of our Lord not only become more comprehensible, but acquire the background and frame in which they develop in their entire ''breadth, length and depth,'' as words of eternal life. Think, for instance, of the words accompanying the washing of the feet at Holy Thursday Mass, the words of the Sermon on the Mount at the Mass on All Saints' Day, or those of the Gospel of Pentecost.

The Liturgy also conveys the direct consciousness of the value of communion as such. I mean the notion that communion is not valuable only insofar as the sanctification of each individual is concerned—a thesis which has been advanced all too often—but also because it is precious and valuable in itself, because God is imitated and glorified in it. The loving communion of the faithful not only engenders the sanctity of the individual person, but it is also the precious fruit of that sanctity, as it is mysteriously revealed in the words of Christ to His disciples: ''By this shall all men know that you are my disciples, if you have love for one another.'' The communion of saints implies a separate new value in addition to that of individual saintliness, a value that would be lacking if the world consisted only of saints in no way linked together.

This value of unity as such, and of the victory of love which is manifested in communion, apart from all that it means for individual sanctification, is revealed to us in many passages of the Liturgy, especially in the Epistles of St. Paul and in the Psalm, ''Behold how good and how pleasant it is for brethren to dwell together in unity (*Ecce quam bonum et quam jucundum habitare fratres in unum*).''

Apart from this particular value of communion, we behold here *a new dimension of the glorification of God*. ''When two or three are gathered together'' in the name of Christ, there appears a new dimension of the lordship of Christ, different from the case in which two persons separate and not linked together adhere to Christ. Of course, the most important thing is the lordship of Christ in each individual soul. But the communion of the Mystical Body of Christ presents its own dimension of the lordship of God and the

glorification of God, which is different from the lordship of God in the individual soul—and this quite
apart from the fact that the soul of the individual can
be ontologically bound to Christ only by becoming a
member of His Mystical Body. On the obverse side, a
pseudocommunity of heretics represents a new evil
over and above the mere sum of heretics who are not
bound together, for this pseudocommunity increases
the outrage in the eyes of God.

And the Liturgy is fully and directly awake to this
particular value of the kingdom of God, of the *chorus*
of prayer, praise and glorification, beyond the individual prayers of the faithful. This increase of value
is not made in terms of numbers and it must not be
identified with quantitative categories according to
which the individual, being one, appears as far too
insignificant. The individual in whom Christ lives is
also infinitely precious in the eyes of God: ''Precious
in the sight of God is the death of his saints.'' The increase of values stems rather from the interpersonal
lordship of Christ in the kingdom of Christ, which is
added to the realm of lordship in the individual soul.
Fundamentally speaking these are all simply different
aspects of the one essential fact of the Mystical Body
of Christ. It is obvious that through the Liturgy we
constantly grow into this unity and are constantly
reminded of it as nowhere else.

The unique character of communion of the Mystical
Body of Christ is first of all embodied in the liturgical
act, in the celebration of the holy Sacrifice of the Mass
and in the recitation of the Office. I do not speak here

of the ontological supernatural formation of all into one, which is accomplished in the unbloody representation of the Sacrifice on the Cross, of the streams of divine love which objectively put an end to all the divisions and conflicts brought about by sin in man. I mean the ultimate ''We'' which binds the faithful, the priests and Christ to one another, in the offering of holy Mass, the ''We'' which reaches its climax in the common meal at the Lord's table. All receive the one body of the Lord, all are assimilated into the one Lord. Even if we leave aside the supreme ontological supernatural unity which is realized here, the very act of undergoing this experience represents an incomparable communion-forming power.

And the prayer in common, the self-constituted ''We'' which is uttered when God is to be praised, thanked or implored, the gesture of the Divine Office as such, is a fulfillment of the communion of the Mystical Body of Christ, an actualization of that deepest, uttermost bond of love, and of the common destiny of guilt, atonement and sonship in Christ. One faith, one hope, one love, one longing, one expectation of the day of our Lord! One vigil, one joy, one praise! Everything is drawn into the ultimate unity in God. And this ultimate character of communion expressed in the Liturgy appears also in the meaning and atmosphere of its individual words and thoughts, as, for instance, in the spontaneous plural of the ''*Gaudete* (Rejoice),'' of the ''Let us all rejoice as we celebrate this feast (*Gaudeamus omnes diem festem celebrantes*),'' of the Gloria of the holy Mass (''We praise Thee, we bless Thee, we adore Thee, we glorify Thee''), of the ''Brethren: be sober, be watchful (*Fratres, sobrii estote et vigilate*),'' of the Pater noster, and innumerable other passages.

Let us also recall the prayer *Communicantes* before the Consecration and the ''*Nobis quoque peccatoribus*'' after the Consecration, as well as the Secret of the Feast of Corpus Christi: ''Grant to Thy Church the gifts of unity and peace, which are mystically signified by the gifts which we offer up.'' Or, again, the Antiphon during the washing of the feet on Holy Thursday: ''Where charity and love is, there God is. / The love of Christ hath gathered us together in one. / Let us rejoice and be glad in Him.' / Let us fear and love the living God. / And let us love Him with a sincere heart. / When therefore we are gathered together in one, / Let us take heed not to be divided in mind. / Let malicious quarrels cease, let all strife cease. / And let Christ our God be in the midst of us. (*Ubi caritas et amor, Deus ibi est. / Congregavit nos in unum Christi amor. / Exsultemus, et in ipso jucundemur. / Timeamus et amemus Deum vivum. / Et ex corde diligamus nos sincero. / Simul ergo cum in unum congregamur: / Ne nos mente dividamur, caveamus. / Cessent jurgia maligna, cessent lites. / Et in medio nostri sit Christus Deus*).''

In this spirit of communion embodied in the Liturgy we find one of the most fundamental traits of true personality. An isolated man, one who has not become conscious of the ultimate objective link binding him to all other men before God, is an unawakened, immature, even a mutilated man. That liberal conception which considers the "solitary" man as the great, profound human being is the logical outcome of the understanding of communion as something peripheral in its nature. Of course, a true personality is, in one sense, solitary among average men, because this personality is alone in his knowledge of that deep communion to which average men have not awakened; he is not satisfied with the superficialities of mere interest or pleasure and seeks a profounder link; he does not inwardly accept the communion offered by the average. But a true personality is never solitary in the sense of being isolated from others in the depths, in the sense of indifference or hostility; he is not unalive to that ultimate, triumphant unity with his brother, whom he sees in the place where each man in truth stands before God, whether he is aware of it or not. The fathers of the desert and the hermits lived entirely in that spirit of true communion, unlike their pagan contemporaries inhabiting crowded cities, surrounded by other men and bound to them by peripheral ties. The true measure of the depth of a man will much rather be found in whether or not he is awakened to that spirit of true communion, in whether or not there has been a breaking-down of the inner walls of self-assertion, in the defenses of the sphere of his ego.

The shutting up of oneself in this inner fortress of isolation, which exists secretly even in the most jovial joiner of clubs, is proof of narrowness, limitation, even stupidity. For it presupposes a certain egocentric attitude toward the world and God. The man who has been melted by the sun of values, and above all the man who has been wounded by the love of Christ, is also lovingly open to every man and has entered into the objective unity of all. Yes, this ultimate true spirit of communion, the universal disposition to love, and the life in the ultimate loving "We," is only possible as a fruit of the ultimate "I-thou-communion" with Christ, through which we are transfigured into Christ. Every attempt to achieve this "We" without Christ leads to a superficially anchored pseudo-communion. It suffices to recall, for instance, the humanitarian ideal. Every attempt to achieve a "We" which does not pass through the "thou" of the God-man, fails to achieve the full conquest of egocentricity; on the contrary, it leads to a mass-egoism, which is perhaps even lower than the egoism of the individual, in its pretension to be an ultimate liberation from the imprisonment of self.

Thus we see that the Liturgy draws us quite obviously and organically into that true spirit of communion which is the indispensable foundation of true personality. It leads us through Christ to the "I-thou" communion with our brother and to the ultimate "We-communion" of humanity in the Mystical Body of Christ. In itself it leads us through Christ into the presence of God, where there is no more *isolation* and no more separation. It is not only true that the Liturgy teaches us about this communion; that, in addition, it offers it to us as a commandment; but in the Liturgy this communion actually lives, it is *there*, in the common adoring sacrifice, praise and prayer, and in the common reception of God's grace, all *per Christum Dominum nostrum*.

V

The Spirit of Reverence in the Liturgy

A man is rich in values, is a personality, in the highest sense of the word, to the degree that he perceives values, that he possesses a spiritual vision clear and open to the fullness of the world of values, above all to the world of supernatural values; to the degree that the gift of himself to the realm of values is pure and absolute, and, above all, to the degree that his self-surrender to Christ, and through Christ to God, is complete. Reverence is the essential basis for such a perception of values and for a true relationship with the whole realm of values, with what is above and what speaks from "above," with the Absolute, the supernatural and the divine. Reverence is the mother of all virtues, of all religion. It is the foundation and the beginning because it enables our spirit to possess real knowledge, and primarily the knowledge of values. It is that fundamental attitude toward being in which one gives all being the opportunity to unfold itself in its specific nature, in which one neither behaves as its master, nor acts toward it in a spirit of familiar conviviality.

In its most primitive form reverence is a response to the general value of being as such, to the dignity which all being (as opposed to nothing or to mere fictitiousness) possesses, to the value of its own consistency, of standing on its own, of the ultimate "positivity" of being. In this right and appropriate attitude toward being as such, this affirmation free from obtrusiveness, this silent, contemplative disposition toward being as being, the world begins to disclose itself in its entire depth, differentiation, and plenitude of value. Every newly-disclosed value creates a new form, enrichment, and differentiation of reverence. So, too, every newly-evolved form of reverence, and consequently, every new response of reverence to the newly-disclosed values opens and widens our outlook, enabling us to grasp new values and to understand better those which are already known. Reverence is thus the foundation of all perception and sense of values. But it is also an indispensable element of every response to value; or, in other words, it is a fundamental component of a true relationship with the world of values. It represents the proper answer to the majesty of values, to the "message" they convey to us of God, of the absolute, the infinitely superior. Only the person who possesses reverence is capable of real enthusiasm, of joy insofar as it is motivated by values, true love, and obedience. The man who lacks reverence is blind to values and incapable of submission to them.

The lack of reverence may have two roots, and accordingly there are two different types of men wanting in reverence: the arrogant person and the senseless, blunt one. The root of the first is to be found in pride. The man who lacks reverence because of pride and arrogance approaches everything with conceit and presumption, imagines that he knows everything, that he sees through everything. He is interested in the world only insofar as it serves his self-glorification, insofar as it enhances his own importance. He does not take being seriously in itself and he leaves things no spiritual room to unfold their own essences. He thinks himself always greater than that which is not himself. The world holds no mystery for him. He treats everything tactlessly, with easy familiarity, and everything seems to him to be at his disposal. To his insolent, conceited gaze, to his despotic approach, the world is sealed, silent, stripped of all mystery, deprived of all depth, flat and limited to one dimension. He stands in desolate emptiness, blind to all the values and secrets of being, circling endlessly around himself.

There is however another form of irreverence, one which is born of concupiscence. The concupiscent man is interested in the world only as a means in procuring pleasure for himself. His is a dominating position in the face of being, not because he wills domination as such, but because he wants to use being for his pleasure. He, too, circles around in the narrowness of his own self. He does not face the world with arrogance and conceit, but with a blunt stupidity. Stubbornly imprisoned in his own self, he violates being, and seeing it only from the outside, he thus misses its true meaning. To this type also of the irreverent man the world refuses to disclose its breadth, height, and depth, its richness of values and mysteries.

The reverent man, the man who is disposed to know something higher than himself and his pleasure, and wills to submit to it and abandon himself, the man who grasps his metaphysical situation and lives it, is not only capable of perceiving values and open to the mysteries of being. Such a man is also open first of all to the Absolute; in other words, he does not shut himself off from the Fact of all Facts, from the existence of God, the absolute lord. Without this reverence, there is no religion, not even primitive, natural religion. Reverence is not an attitude like humility which can appear only in confrontation with the true image of God, as reflected in the Face of Christ and presented to us by the Church. Reverence is, at least in its primitive form, the presupposition of faith, a *praeambulum fidei*. In antiquity, we find a deep reverence not only in Socrates and Plato, but also in the ethos of the people. How deep was the consciousness of the unrighteousness which lies in *hubris*, in that failure of reverence, in that unbridled self-assertion, in that loud and false security!

For humility, on the contrary, there is no place in the ancient conception of the world. The ancient fear of God which the Scriptures say is the beginning of wisdom (*initium sapientiae timor Domini*) in itself presupposes this fundamental attitude of reverence.

Reverence in its primitive form is not only the basis of every religion, and, above all, of the receptiveness to the *lumen Christi*, to the word of God; but it is also a constitutive element of faith, hope, and love of God. Complete, fully-ripened reverence is a component of a true relationship with God, and specifically with the God of Revelation. How often, even in a religious man, do we find mixed in with his relations to God a certain self-relishing—so clearly shown wherever the relationship to God is a sentimental one—or else a certain familiarity with God, a false, clumsy complacency. There are also cases in which such trivial categories as mere formal loyalty, correctness, and propriety are insinuated into the relation with God, the eternal, all-holy and inscrutable.

All this means a lack of reverence. The significance of reverence for the full personality can easily be grasped. The greatest natural ''endowment,'' the greatest latitude of talents and capacities can never lead to true personality if reverence is lacking. For the latter is the basis of the second essential component of personality, the perceiving of values, an organic contact with the world of values, and most ultimate of all, the dying to oneself, the preparation of inner room for Christ.

Liturgy and Personality

The man without reverence is necessarily flat and limited. This lack is an essential mark of stupidity. Even he whose mind is obdurate and helpless, but who possesses reverence, does not manifest that offensive, tactlessly persistent stupidity of which it is said that "even the gods struggle against it in vain." The lack of reverence is a specific defect of our modern age. On the one hand, the feeling of reverence is undermined by the increasing technicalization and instrumentalization of the world wherein everything is considered only as a means for the attainment of practical aims, and being is not allowed to be taken seriously. On the other hand, the attitude of self-glorification is increased in man by progress in the knowledge of secondary causes and by the conquest of the physical world. This makes us forget that "He has made us and we have not made ourselves." It makes the shortsighted intoxicated with superficial knowledge so that they overlook the *causa prima* because of the *causae secundae*. Herein lies a specific "fatuity." Here the spirit of irreverence manifests itself, the "short circuit" of the spirit to which the irreverent man falls victim. According to this ultimate criterion, the most primitive people who ignore all *causae secundae* and link everything directly to God, the *causa prima*, are infinitely closer to truth than the modern man who has ceased to perceive the deepest meaning and basis of all things because he is completely absorbed by all that is secondary. In this ultimate sense, the irreverent modern man, in spite of all his knowledge, is far more "stupid" than the most primitive savage possessing reverence. To this fading away of reverence is linked the peculiar triteness and leveling of our entire life.

Yet it is not the ethos of reverence as such which is the decisive point, but reverence as an adequate response to the true God.

This true reverence is not the misty reverence of a vague imitation as found in primitive people; it is not the reverence inspired by the rustle of holy trees or by an immersion into the biological, seemingly more powerful than ourselves. Still less is it the pseudo-reverence expressed in different pantheisms, the shrinking consciousness of an immensity in which we are but a drop. It is not even the noble reverence of a Socrates before the daimon, or of a Plato, which is only an expectation, an obscure questioning, fading away in the All. We are speaking of enlightened reverence which clearly grasps its object and is formed by the latter's infinite and manifest greatness, its mysterious, inconceivable depths, and by the infinite fullness of its values.

The Liturgy is penetrated more than anything else by the spirit of true reverence, and it draws those who live it directly into this spirit. The right fundamental relation to God and to creation lives in all its parts, and it leads to the classical attitude toward God through Christ. It is deeply permeated by the fear of God, by the *cum timore et tremore*, and at the same time by the consciousness that we are sons of God, in which we cry out ''Abba, Father!'' It is full of the spirit of *servire Domino in laetitia*, of serving

Liturgy and Personality

God in joy. In the beginning of Matins, the Church prays the Invitatory. This Psalm vividly presents before our mind our own nothingness before God's majesty, our absolute dependence on Him, the fact that we belong to Him; and, moreover, in praying it, we live the truth.

"For the Lord is a great God, and a great king above all gods. For in His hands are all the ends of the earth: and the heights of the mountains are His. / For the sea is His, and He made it: and His hands formed the dry land. Come, let us adore and fall down before God: let us weep before the Lord Who made us. For He is the Lord our God: and we are His people and the sheep of His pasture (*Quoniam Deus magnus Dominus, et Rex magnus super omnes deos: quoniam non repellet Dominus plebem suam, quia in manu ejus sunt omnes fines terrae, et altitudines montium ipse conspicit. / Quoniam ipsius est mare, et ipse fecit illud, et aridam fundaverunt manus ejus: venite adoremus et procidamus ante Deum: ploremus coram Domino, qui fecit nos, quia ipse est Dominus Deus noster: nos autem populus ejus, et oves pascuae ejus).*"

The entire Liturgy is pervaded with this reverence before the *majestas Domini*, the clear consciousness of His absolute dominion, and the acknowledgment that we receive all from Him. And yet this attitude has no Jansenist or Calvinist note of remoteness from God, of being crushed by God's greatness, no annihilating disdain for ourselves: rather its spirit is that of "I will go in unto the altar of God, unto God Who giveth joy to my youth (*Introibo ad altare Dei, ad*

Deum, qui laetificat juventutem meam).'' This attitude is
one which finds its expression in ''For His mercy
endureth forever (*Quoniam in aeternum misericordia
ejus*),'' in ''Taste and see how sweet is the Lord (*Gustate et videte quam suavis est Dominus*),'' in ''I shall
sing through all eternity the mercies of the Lord (*Misericordia Domini cantabo in aeternum*).'' Let us recall the
upward glance which marks the beginning of each
day, the ''O God, come to my assistance, O Lord
make haste to help me (*Deus in adjutorium meum intende, Domine ad adjuvandum me festina*).'' When these
words are sung, how especially are we enveloped in
the deepest reverence before God and drawn into the
true situation of the creature in relation to God. We
are drawn into the rhythm of reverence of the praying Church. How strong is the spirit of reverence in
the Prefaces and in the Sanctus!—a reverence which
is at the same time linked to the consciousness that
we are sons of God. The spirit of reverence is also expressed in the fact that in all liturgical prayers (*ora-
tiones*) we never turn directly to the Father, but
always address Him through the One in Whom alone
God is well pleased: *per Christum Dominum nostrum.*
This feeling, that we only dare address God in Christ
and through Christ, is one which is deeply opposed to
all easy familiarity; it never allows us to forget the awe
in which we must always make our approach to God.

The holy Sacrifice of the Mass is especially penetrated with this spirit: the necessity of sacrificing to
God, the impossibility of offering Him an adequate
sacrifice because of our poverty, the sacrificial

prayer of Christ in which we are allowed to participate, the primal, classical attitude before God, ''By
Him, and with Him, and in Him, is to Thee God the
Father almighty, in the unity of the Holy Ghost, all
honor and glory (*Per ipsum, cum ipso, et in ipso est tibi,
Deo Patri omnipotenti, in unitate Spiritus Sancti, omnis
honor et gloria*).''

We find this spirit, too, toward all that enters into
contact with the Lord's holy Body, in the handling of
the paten and the cleansing of the chalice. We also
find it in all that symbolizes Christ or is dedicated to
the divine service, in the kissing of the divine altar
and the Gospel book. It is expressed in the bodily
comportment of the priest, the faithful and the religious; in the standing up during the reading of the
Gospel, during the songs of praise taken from the
Gospels, the Magnificat, Benedictus, Nunc dimittis,
in the bowing of the head during the Gloria Patri. The
very fact of the harmonious structure and order of the
entire Liturgy, extending even to the outer comportment, contains a profound element of reverence. This
unique organic structure, corresponding so clearly to
the adequate inner attitude of one who is standing
before God, is the very opposite of slackness; and, in
equal measure, it is opposed to the attitude of a military or athletic drill.

He who lives in the Liturgy becomes filled with reverence not only in the sense of that fundamental reverence which is a *praeambulum fidei*, a precondition of
faith, but also in the sense of that reverence which is a
part of faith in the Triune God, hope in God, love of

God—in other words, of the reverence of the God-man Jesus Christ Himself.

The formation of personality by the Liturgy, as explained here, means not only the molding of what is most central in the human person, his right relation toward God. It also means the molding of right relations toward all realms of being and every kind of value. It means the formation of the whole man. Even when we are concerned with realms of being not expressly mentioned in the Liturgy our right attitude toward God must serve us as a *causa exemplaris*, a model for our attitude toward all values.

The man formed by the Liturgy is reverent toward his neighbor, in whom he sees (if this latter is a member of the Mystical Body of Christ) a "second Christ" or (if he is not yet "reborn") a soul destined to be thus reborn and transformed into Christ. The words of Christ, "As long as you did it to one of these my least brethren, you did it to me," disclose to us the entire world of holy, reverence-inspiring plenitude which lives in every Christian. Above all, the human being acquires an extraordinary dignity through the Incarnation of the eternal Word, the Second Divine Person. It may be said that our faith in Christ leads us directly to this reverence for man. Whoever lives the true Catholic faith—whether or not he is familiar with the Liturgy—certainly possesses this reverence for his neighbor. Surely, the Liturgy does not teach us anything new beyond that which is already included in the Credo. But the Liturgy is accomplished faith, lived faith. It plunges us into the full reality of the truth of faith; it creates the spiritual space in which the world of faith, or, more correctly, the world disclosed by faith, penetrates every pore of our being, in which we breathe the supernatural air; it brings us to the ultimate reality which, in the holy Sacrifice of the Mass and in the sacraments, we even touch ontologically. It builds up that sacred sense of communion, already described, which is entirely steeped in reverence. The unifying power here is Christ Himself, and our link with other men necessarily implies our reverent response to our brother as a vessel of grace.

There are certain nonliturgical forms of community among the faithful where, in spite of a common faith, the plane on which we unite is quite distinct from the supernatural. In numerous Catholic associations, despite their high practical significance, fellowship is too often born out of social or professional interests; their atmosphere is made up of coziness and smugness, joviality, jollity, in which *the other* is considered as playing a social role, as a comrade, a "buddy," or at best as one sharing the same "view of life." The abundance and depth of the spiritual person, as a creature made in the image of God, and especially "membership" in the Mystical Body of Christ and the fact of being sons of God are effaced in their consciousness and do not play the part of a real, accomplished element in the sense of communion. In such unions the spirit of reverence toward our brothers cannot be formed in us, the kind of spirit which we directly acquire in the Liturgy and which rings out to us in the Epistle of Easter Saturday: "But you are a chosen generation, a kingly priesthood, a holy nation, a purchased people."

The man formed by the Liturgy is also reverent toward his own body. He regards it as "the temple of the Holy Ghost." This simple truth of supernatural life is achieved in the Liturgy. Let us recall the rites of baptism, confirmation, holy anointing, and extreme unction.

This attitude of reverence is especially opposed to all pragmatic conduct. The contrary of a reverent attitude toward being results when everything is considered only as a means, as an instrument for subjective and fortuitous aims; when all is used as a coin for which something can be exchanged; when nothing is taken seriously for its own sake; when nothing is ever conceived in its function of imitating God, in its inner nobility, in its objective, God-willed vocation, its destiny to serve the higher.

The Liturgy naturally leads us to an attitude of reverence toward pure matter, in its great classical display of all things in *conspectu Dei*. The Liturgy considers all things (water, fire, wax, bread, wine, oil, salt, the sea, the mountains) as images of an endless fullness of God in their inner preciousness and also in their mysterious symbolism in the supernatural order.

A unique perspective of the cosmos appears each time the Liturgy speaks expressly of a created thing: the industrious bee in the Exsultet of Holy Saturday; water and fire in the rites of their blessing. A new dimension of depth is disclosed in these created things, a dimension quite different from the blunt one we are accustomed to in our daily lives. They are aglow with the light of that mystery of the heights which inhabits every being, in that it has been created by God, and has felt the sacred touch of His finger. This perspective is the fertile ground for a deep reverence toward each individual thing—in accordance with the hierarchy of being and values—and toward the cosmos as a whole.

VI

The Spirit of Response-to-Value in the Liturgy

We have already seen that the second component in the formation of personality consists in the perceiving of value and in the person's fundamental response-to-value. To express it in other words, this second foundation of the formation of personality and of the transformation into Christ is in the conscious, meaningful relation to the world, manifesting itself in the apprehension of, and the response to, value. To be irradiated and affected by values, to affirm and give oneself up to all things that possess a value, and to be joyous and enthusiastic over them, above all to love them, is to be wed to the world of values; thereby we become transformed and the fullness of personal values blossoms out in us. In the adoring love of the God Who disclosed Himself in Christ we become like

Christ; the life of Christ ontologically implanted in us by baptism develops personally in us.

The very soul of the response-to-value is the consciousness that an adequate response is due to each value according to its rank. The motive of the response-to-value should never be the desire to bring about the transformation of the person, but to give to the value its due response.

This was seen before when the aim with which the Liturgy is performed was examined. One of the most elementary truths is involved here. It may be expressed as follows: To every value an adequate response is due on the part of the person *because it is a value*. This response should not be given in order that something may come out of it or be realized through it. Nor should it be given in the name of this or that purpose. Indeed, there is an ultimate, cosmic value in the suitable response to every value, and an ultimate cosmic ''disvalue,'' a disharmony, in the lack of response or in a false response. This cosmic value has nothing to do with the personal value involved in the right response. The personal value is something new beyond the value represented by the fact that the right response is given, and indeed presupposes this cosmic value. The cosmic ''disvalue'' exists even when a value—a moral person, for instance—does not receive the adequate response of love and respect because it is misunderstood through no fault of the one who misunderstands. The cosmic value of the objective fact that everything possessing a value should receive an adequate response of will, of joy, enthusiasm, and love according to the kind of value it represents, finds its highest, ultimate *causa exemplaris* in the eternal loving response between the First and Second Divine Persons.

This primary fact that to every value an adequate response is due on the part of the person, because the value is such as it is, cannot be demonstrated or deduced from something else; it is something ultimate which we can only apprehend directly. This primary fact finds its highest expression in the response-to-value of adoring love and glorification of God Who includes all values.

One of the most essential elements of true personality is the consciousness that we owe to values a due response. By this the *theocentric* man is distinguished from the *egocentric* one. Shut up in himself, the egocentric man is incapable of this self-abandon. He is incapable of giving himself up to the world of meaning and value, simply for its own sake and for no other reason, in unison with the objective logos. The purely egocentric man, dominated entirely by pride or concupiscence, is generally blind to values, has no contact with them and their inner life, and is also without contact with God Who includes all values. The proud man is hostile to values. The concupiscent man is indifferent to them. The proud man hates God and denies Him expressly in an impotent revolt. The concupiscent man ignores God.

But there exist less extreme forms of self-centeredness. Among them is the type of man who is capable of perceiving values and penetrating them, but whose dominant interest is nevertheless at all times centered on himself. He will never obey the demand of giving a suitable response-to-value simply because such a response is due to it for no other reason. He will help another man only in order to grow morally himself and not in the name of love. He approaches beauty in order to attain spiritual culture. He adores God in order to achieve religious progress. Of course, our own person also demands that we should manifest toward it a responding-to-value interest, that we should affirm the immanent design of God in us and seek its full development. We must first of all affirm the supernatural life bestowed on us through baptism and seek its full unfolding. But this precisely means to be responsive to values, to fix our gaze only on the value confronting us, and to live wholly in it; it means that we do not isolate the moral significance from the morally relevant value at stake, and, still more, that we do not cast a sidelong glance, do not "squint" in order to perceive the act of response at the same moment in which it is being given to the value. Here it is of no importance whether we ourselves, another man, an event, or a thing are the objects of this response. When we reject our own negative-values in contrition and at the same time "revoke" our past unworthy conduct, our comportment is as objectively directed as in loving another human being. Contrariwise, the egocentric man, in manifesting contrition, casts a sidelong glance and "squints" at his own contrition; he will even "relish" his moral attitude instead of being absorbed in the sorrow he experiences because of his past conduct. While examining his conscience, he will take satisfaction in his piety.

When this egocentric type encounters a value, as in beholding something beautiful or meeting a noble man, he will see in all this but an opportunity for ascetic exercises, instead of taking interest in the value as such, responding to it as a reflection of God, and forgetting himself and giving himself up to God who speaks to us after His own fashion in all true values. This egocentric type will help his neighbor, not because this help is due to him, nor because he must testify to the truth that the hungry and thirsting Christ stands before him, but because he seeks to accomplish a meritorious act. The egocentric type does not adore God because the glory of God brings him to his knees, because God is infinitely glorious, inconceivably holy and great, nor because he understands that this response is due to the King of Eternal Glory. He adores God because he wants to become more perfect, to acquire merits and gain graces. In short, somehow the egocentric man transforms his giving himself up to value into a means for his own perfection; he is not interested in this perfection because of the glorification of God but because it is his *own* perfection.

The more free from this self-centeredness a man is, the more he is a personality. Every form of self-centeredness, of being shut up in oneself, is narrowness, pettiness, limitation, a cutting-off of oneself from the sources of all true life, indeed from God Himself. The egocentric tendency empties all response-to-value of its content, desubstantializes it, destroys the wedding to values, and hence blocks the inner transformation of the person, the richness in values which the person acquires through response-to-value and from it.

The egocentric type is in a tragic situation. For he will never achieve his own fullness of values which he seeks, demands and wants to enjoy. The more he demands, the less will he obtain. For only when the response-to-value is given to its object, purely because it is a value, can this fullness in values be achieved, only when the person is penetrated with the consciousness that this response is objectively due to the value. Such a fullness in values can be achieved only through self-forgetfulness, by not instrumentalizing the response-to-value, by not "squinting" at the fullness achieved by the self, "letting not thy left hand know what thy right hand doeth," according to the Gospel.

To such men may be applied the words of Christ, "Amen I say to you, they have received their reward." In the utterance, "He that shall lose his life shall find it," shines the exalted truth that the person is rich in values to the extent that he gives himself up in pure response to the world of values, and first of all to God who contains all values. A man is more of a personality, in the highest sense of the word, the less he seeks to turn life into an "art," the less he is concerned directly with the development of his own personality. He is the more a true personality, the more he progresses in giving himself up to values, and especially in self-forgetfulness and complete donation to God. The creative primary gesture of personality-formation is the pure gift of oneself to the value for its own sake, without the commingling of anything egocentric.

In the Liturgy we find embodied in a unique fashion the spirit of true response-to-value, this awareness (the antithesis of egocenteredness) that an adequate answer is due to value because it is such as it is. Not in the name of this or that aim, nor in order to achieve improvement or sanctification of ourselves, but because "Thou only art Holy. Thou only art Lord. Thou only art Most High. (*Quoniam tu solus Sanctus, tu solus Dominus, tu solus Altissimus*)." Before the Gospel we say, "Glory to You, O Lord (*Gloria tibi, Domine*)." Before the Preface we say, "Let us give thanks to the Lord, our God (*Gratias agamus Domino, Deo nostro*)"; and the answer is "It is truly meet and just (*Vere dignum et justum est*)." And at the end of the Canon: "By Him, and with Him, and in Him, is to Thee, God the Father almighty, in the unity of the Holy Ghost, all honor and glory (*Per ipsum et cum ipso et in ipso est tibi, Deo Patri omnipotenti, in unitate Spiritus Sancti, omnis honor et gloria*)."

Above all else, the holy Sacrifice of the Mass as a whole is the supreme fulfillment of adoration and love which gives itself and sacrifices itself completely. The sacrificial love of the God-man, the gift of Himself to the heavenly Father, is the primal theocentric attitude. And to the extent that a man is inwardly formed through participation in the holy Sacrifice of the Mass, all egocentric deviation from response-to-value is bound to disappear. The spirit which breathes in the holy Mass is penetrated with the fundamental fact that the response of adoring and atoning love is due to God's endless majesty and holiness. Likewise the various thoughts and words in the holy Mass are penetrated with this truth. The Gloria clearly expresses it: "We give Thee thanks for Thy great glory (*Gratias agimus tibi propter magnam gloriam tuam*)."

The Divine Office as a whole also testifies to the primary fact that we owe God this expressed glorification, *propter magnam gloriam tuam*. The individual parts likewise are penetrated with this idea that we owe praise, glory, and thanks to God; they convey the inner significance of this response which in no way bears the character of a means. This pure glorification is seen, first of all, in the "Glory be to the Father and to the Son and to the Holy Spirit (*Gloria Patri et Filio, et Spiritui Sancto*)" which marks all the Hours of the day; it is also seen in "O Lord, Thou wilt open my lips; and my mouth shall declare Thy praise (*Domine, labia mea aperies; et os meum annuntiabit laudem tuam*)," in the "Come, let us adore and fall down before God (*Venite, adoremus, et procidamus ante Deum*)" from the Invitatory Psalm, in the Te Deum at the end of Matins, in the Song of Praise of the three youths in the fiery furnace, in the "Laudate" Psalms at Lauds, in the Benedictus at Lauds, in the Magnificat at Vespers, and in innumerable other passages of the Psalms and Antiphons. Suffice it to recall "O praise the Lord, all ye nations (*Laudate Dominum omnes gentes*)," "Praise the Lord, ye children (*Laudate pueri Dominum*)," "Come, bless the Lord (*Ecce nunc benedicite Dominum*)" from Compline, "How admirable is Thy name in the whole earth (*Quam admirabile est nomen tuum in universa terra*)," "How great are Thy works, O Lord! (*Quam magnificat sunt opera tua Domine*)," and many, many others. The doxology concluding every hymn conveys in the most express manner the consciousness that this response is due to God. The same can be said of "To You we owe praise, to You we owe our hymn of praise (*Te decet laus, te decet hymnus*)" at the end of monastic Matins.

The person formed by the Liturgy has absorbed in his flesh and blood the notion that he owes a suitable response to every value. He will rejoice in every exalted spectacle of nature, the beauty of the starlit sky, the majesty of the sea and mountains, the charm of life, the world of plants and animals, the nobility of a profound truth, the mysterious glow of a man's purity, the victorious goodness of a fervent love of neighbor. The man formed by the Liturgy will affirm all this as a reflection of the eternal glory of God, and not with the thought that it is meant for his own satisfaction or that through such an affirmation he will develop and grow inwardly. It will be on his part a spontaneous accomplishment of what is due, the realization of the fact that he owes this response to all that has value, that the value in question objectively

"deserves" this response. It will be not the fulfillment of a painful duty, but a spontaneous gift of
himself to the value, a blissful acquiescence in the
lovable beauty of the value, a gladdening submission
to the Lord of whom it is said "Taste and see how
sweet the Lord is (*Gustate et videte quam suavis est
Dominus*)." The person formed by the Liturgy will
not ask himself whether he is obliged under sin to
give this response. His entire value-responding attitude, his heart and spirit will be turned completely
toward the world of values and God in the first place.
By this he will speak: "I have sought Thy face, O
Lord (*Vultum tuum quaesivi, Domine*)." He will achieve
this response freely from within, and even experience
it as the highest of all bliss.

Here it should be understood that the awareness of
the fact that an adequate response is due to each
value, that it does not depend on our arbitrary choice
whether we give a response and what response we
give (as for example it depends on our choice
whether we prefer a warm or cold room), that this
awareness goes hand in hand with the attraction of
the glow of values, the "enchantment" inspired by
the inner beauty of values. This awareness of the
world of values and ultimately of God, of owing a response of love and joy, has nothing to do with any
neutral feeling of duty that goes against the heart's
inclination; it is organically bound up with the longing for union with each thing that possesses value
and speaks to us of the glory of God, and especially
with the longing for union with God Himself. Such a

longing is an essential element of every response-to-value, and primarily of love.

The full conforming to values, as it is expressed above all in the central response-to-value of love, implies not only the affirmation of the value in itself, the "We give You thanks for Your great glory (*Gratias agimus tibi propter magnam gloriam tuam*)," but also the longing for union with the object of value, the spiritual "hastening" toward the beloved, in which the unique giving up of one's own person is achieved. And just this *full* response-to-value is *due* to God. The "*Vultum tuum quaesivi* (I have sought Thy face, O Lord)" must build itself up organically on the "*Gratias agimus tibi propter magnam gloriam tuam.*" Otherwise the response-to-value would not be complete. To see a selfish motive behind this longing for union would be to fall victim to a grave error. It would imply the failure to see clearly how this longing grows necessarily out of pure value-responsiveness, and how the giving of oneself can only find its fulfillment in this longing. Of course, here also an inner sequence must be observed. In the first place there must be the pure response-to-value affirmation which appears in its highest form in loving adoration, from which "the serving of God" flows forth. Then only does the turning toward union follow. It must be stressed that the *intentio unionis* manifests itself not only in *longing*—that is, in the situation where the union is not yet achieved—but also in unfading delight in the possession, a delight which is to be continued in eternity, where "all is fulfilled." It is a specific lack of classicism, a lack of understanding of the ultimate, organic relationships to see an egocentric element in this striving toward union which essentially belongs to love. The Liturgy teaches us that this striving belongs to the true relationship to God; that, further, the *intentio unionis* is *due* to God; that God demands from us not only adoration but also love; and that He Himself loves us with this love. The longing to touch God, the will to attain to Him, is not only a profoundly legitimate element of the liturgical act, it is even necessary for the full glorification of God. This loving motion is essentially embedded in the glorification which the God-man renders to His heavenly Father.

The eternal union with God is also a theme of the Liturgy. It suffices to recall the already mentioned *"Quaesivi vultum tuum"* of the Sunday within the Octave of the Ascension, or "One thing I have asked of the Lord, this will I seek after; that I may dwell in the house of the Lord all the days of my life (*Unam petii a Domino, hanc requiram, ut inhabitem in domo Domini omnibus diebus vitae meae*)," or "My soul panteth after Thee (*Sitivit in te anima mea*)," and "As the hart panteth after the fountains of water, so my soul panteth after Thee, O God. My soul hath thirsted after the strong living God. When shall I come and appear before the face of God?" All of Advent is penetrated with this loving longing which is so movingly expressed by St. John in the concluding words of the Apocalypse: "Come, Lord Jesus (*Veni Domine Jesu*)." This loving longing grows ever more intense until it reaches the "Drop down dew, ye heavens (*Rorate coeli desuper*)" and the "Come, O Lord, and do not delay (*Veni Domine et noli tardare*)" of the Fourth Sunday of Advent.

But this element manifests itself especially in holy Communion in which the God-man comes to us in an ineffable manner and unites Himself to us in a way which is far beyond all the possibilities of natural union: "He that eateth My flesh, and drinketh My blood abideth in Me, and I in him (*Qui manducat meam carnem et bibit meum sanguinem, manet in me et ego in eo*)"; "With desire I have desired to eat this pasch with you (*Desiderio desideravi comedere hoc pascha vobiscum*)." And He says this to us in every Communion. But in the Communion of Quinquagesima Sunday the Church sings: "They were not defrauded of that which they craved (*Non sunt fraudati a desiderio suo*)."

It would be an equally gross misunderstanding of the true nature of theocentrism to seek to exclude one's own person as entirely unessential. As we have already seen on different occasions, man must imitate and glorify God through his own being, through the fullness of values which blossom out in him. That Christ should be imitated in a man, and that the unique, unduplicable design of God represented by this man should achieve its complete development, is a great thing in God's eyes. We become strikingly aware of this when we consider what the Credo says: "Who for us men, and for our salvation, came down from heaven (*Qui propter nos homines et propter nostram salutem descendit de coelis*)." What is so extraordinarily significant in the eyes of God should be as significant in our own eyes. It would not be fully and genuinely to "tread before God," sacrifice to Him, adoringly praise Him, glorify Him and pray to Him, if this confrontation between man and God did not take place, a confrontation wherein is put the question: "Who art Thou, and who am I?"

There are defenders of a false theocentrism who believe that one should entirely forget how one is and what one is, in order to rejoice only in the glory of God. This leads to an unserious, one might say, an aestheticized attitude toward God, looking as a spectator upon Him, forgetting that one stands before the Lord of Life and Death, before our Lord, to Whom we belong, to Whom we owe an account. This dropping of one of the partners in the relationship with God is absolutely unclassical. The Liturgy knows nothing of it. Of course our first response to objects of value must be an affirmation of them, a joy in their existence as such. But then the true response-to-value raises the question, "And what about me, can I bear what this value conveys to me of God?" This involves the consciousness of one's own unworthiness and guilt. There are men for whom this last question predominates over all others, so much so that instead of rejoicing in the *magnalia Dei*, the great deeds of God which are revealed in a saint, they feel despondent, saying to themselves: "How different I am! Shall I ever be like him?" This of course is a false and unhealthy attitude. Likewise incorrect is that other attitude wherein we only see the value in itself, without understanding the word which God speaks to us through it, without hearing God's call to us which is also contained in it. The right attitude in contemplating a saint is to rejoice first in the *magnalia Dei*, to experience this joy and gratitude without troubling about what we are ourselves; and then to take into account the word of God which is spoken to us through him, and to say with St. Augustine: "If these, then why not I? (*Si isti cur non ego?*)."

The Liturgy breathes this spirit. In the beginning of the Mass, the priest recites: "I will go in unto the altar of God, to God who gives joy to my youth (*Introibo ad altare Dei, ad Deum qui laetificat juventutem meam*)." Then follows the confrontation with God, the necessary consequence of the true standing before God, the Confiteor, the acknowledgment of one's sins. Only after the appeal to God's mercy—the prayer Misereatur, the asking for forgiveness, and the Kyrie—does the Gloria follow, wherein once more the pure glorification of God is given expression. Before the Gospel, we again hear the prayer of purification uttered by the priest or deacon: "Cleanse my heart and my lips, O God almighty, Who didst cleanse the lips of the prophet Isaias with a live coal (*Munda cor meum ac labia mea, omnipotens Deus, qui labia Isaiae prophetae calculo mundasti ignito*)." Only then does he dare to undertake the reading of the Gospel.

Soon after the Consecration, this confrontation of our soul and God takes place once more in the prayer,

Liturgy and Personality

"To us, also, sinful servants (*Nobis quoque peccatoribus*)." The first part of the Pater noster is but a movement toward God's glory and a full affirmation of this glory in itself, an act of adoration and glorification: "Hallowed be Thy name; Thy kingdom come; Thy will be done (*Sanctificetur nomen tuum; adveniat regnum tuum, fiat voluntas tua*)." This is followed by the second part, in which we pray for the forgiveness of our sins, for our protection and our salvation. After the Pater comes the "Lamb of God, . . . have mercy on us, . . . grant us peace (*Agnus Dei, miserere nobis, dona nobis pacem*)," the "Lord I am not worthy (*Domine non sum dignus*)," and then again the "May it please you (*Placeat tibi*)" before the final blessing, which prayer deals primarily with the glory of God, but closes with the implied reference to our beatitude.

These are not contradictory elements, nor are they two paths lying side by side. They are components of the mutual relationship between man and God in its organic structure, its classical order of attitudes which cannot be separated and which belong to a full, true glorification, all formed from within by the rhythm of glorification.

In the person formed by the Liturgy, in the true personality, the pure response-to-value affirmation of all true values will predominate. He will rejoice and be filled with enthusiasm at the conversion of someone, the nobility of a holy friendship, the exalted character of truth, the beauty of nature, at the greatness and depth of a work of art; he will affirm God's glory reflected in these things and thank the Lord

"because of His great glory." And he will understand that he owes the value the adequate response
which is objectively due to it. But out of this affirmation and understanding there will grow in an organic
way the longing to come into more intimate communion with the good possessing a value, the desire to
enter into the truth, to establish a communion with
the noble person, to be immersed in the beautiful. Of
course, for special reasons, he may renounce this
deeper communion in the name of God, in order to
make place for God alone who contains all values.
But in itself the longing for communion with the
value and with the world of God revealed in it is
linked to the primary rhythm of response-to-value,
the pure affirmation of value in itself. If this were lacking, then the value-responding affirmation would not
be complete and full-blooded, it would be a mere acknowledgment instead of a giving up of oneself.

The complete and genuine man will also understand
the word which God speaks to him in every value, the
call of the "Lift up your hearts (*sursum corda*)" addressed to *him*; he will achieve that confrontation of
himself with values which led St. Peter to exclaim before the revelation of the divine power of Christ: "Depart from me, for I am a sinful man, O Lord!"

So many fail, especially in our days, to hear that
"call" which God addresses to us in every value.
Never in the history of humanity have there been so
many "spectators" of God and of the world of
values. I refer to the people who are enthusiastic
about the Church but do not grasp the "this thing

79

concerns *you* (*tua res agitur*)," which is implied for each of us in the existence of the Church. There are people for example who are full of admiration for a St. Francis of Assisi, but do not realize that their own attitudes and modes of life are so profoundly opposed to those of this saint, and that they should look upon this fact as an intolerable reproach to themselves. Such, too, are those for whom Christ is no longer a scandal, not because they belong to Him and obey His call, but because they live so much as spectators that they no longer undertake any "confrontation" with that which stands before them, because they are deaf to the call of God in His direct "eternal word." Such, too, are those helplessly indifferent aesthetes who slip through our fingers like eels, and can never definitely be grasped, because they affirm all values only as spectators divorced from any consequences for themselves, and they are harder to convert than actual haters of God rising against Him in impotent resentment.

For the man formed by the Liturgy, the pure affirmation of that which has value is organically followed by the longing for union with it, and the confrontation of his self with the world of God present in the value; this affirmation is followed by the understanding of God's call, by the sense of his own unworthiness, by the asking for God's help, and the desire to be transformed. And all this has as its final aim the glorification of God.

However, the decisive feature of true personality is not only the fundamental response-to-value attitude, the living consciousness of the fact that an adequate answer is due to every value, the sense of the objective disharmony implied in every nonresponse-to-value. True personality also demands a clear understanding of the *hierarchy of values*, the preponderance to be given in the response to the greater value, and the renunciation, for its sake, of what is less important. In this inner conformity to the objective order of values lies the secret of true personality. Pettiness, limitation, stupidity, consist precisely in failing to grasp the difference between higher and lower values, between the essential and the less essential; they consist in clinging to the less important and in giving up the more important, acting like Esau when he renounced his birthright for a mess of pottage; the incapacity for renouncing the lesser value for the greater one and abandoning something unimportant in favor of a higher value because the unimportant is so habitual and familiar that it seems impossible to give it up. The great, free personality manifests itself precisely in the fact that like the merchant in the parable of the Gospel he sells everything in order to acquire the single pearl of great price; he freely abandons the habitual and familiar in the name of a higher value, clearly realizes the hierarchy of values, and does not confuse the weight of the habitual with the weight stemming from the rank of the value.

But it is not sufficient that a person should give his preference to the higher value in his action only, in placing only the higher moral demand foremost. His entire attitude toward the world of values must take this hierarchy into account. The admiration and veneration which he offers a value must correspond to its objective height, and so, too, the joy which he feels about something, the place he reserves in his soul for a good. Of what worth is it for a man to be enthusiastic over a masterpiece of art if at the same time he admires as much an insignificant work? Of what worth is it for a person to be enthusiastic about a saint if in the same breath he praises to the same degree an ordinarily meritorious and deserving man? This defective gradation in the order of response desubstantializes the affirmation of the value. If everything is at the same level of the scale, even the greatest enthusiasm over a true value is but a fire made with straw. In placing everything on the same level, such a man remains empty, however much he occupies himself with the world of values, however much he addresses himself to it. The values do not adorn such a man with their nobility; rather they slide off him without clothing him with their spirit.

True perception of value implies the clear grasping of the hierarchy of values. The awareness that a response is due to the value implies necessarily that the response must be an adequate one, and that a higher value demands a response *different* from that which is due to a lower value; it therefore means that the gradation of values is also required on the part of the person. The more inner room a person reserves for the higher values, not letting himself be submerged by the less important ones, and the more he can actualize new dimensions in his soul when the higher values arise before his spiritual eye, so much more is he a genuine *personality*. This is true not only of the attitude toward the values as such, but also of the attitude toward objective goods for the person—freedom, health, liberation from concern about everyday life, respect for one's fellow men, success in professional work, enjoyment of beauty in nature and art, friendship, marriage—insofar as they mean for us a gift of God, and bestow happiness on us. Here also our susceptibility to a certain good, our longing to possess it, must be submitted to a gradation according to the degree of the value implied by the good in question, and the corresponding nobility and depth of its capacity to dispense happiness.

It is above all a sign of deficiency in depth and breadth when a man thinks more of goods which merely procure pleasure (such as good food and drink, the comforts of life, or ownership) than of goods providing spiritual happiness (such as a deeper penetration into truth, contact with the deeper world of beauty in nature and art or a noble communion). When we speak of materialistic (as opposed to *spiritual*) men—men spreading an oppressive and narrowing atmosphere even when they are men of good will from the moral point of view —we mean precisely those whose receptiveness for pleasure-dispensing goods is greater than their receptiveness for happiness-dispensing goods.

But the maintenance of an objective gradation in our attitude toward happiness-dispensing goods is also of decisive significance for the depth and greatness of personality. Limited, indeed, is the man who places his professional work as such, the usual development of his faculties as organizer in a factory or a political party, above the gift of a deep communion of love—he whose soul is more liable to be filled by this and inwardly more attached to it. For of all created goods, the true communion of love with another human being is the highest and noblest one of all, as it is expressed in the words of the Canticle of Canticles: "If a man should give all the substance of his house for love, he shall despise it as nothing."

"The greater the man, the deeper his love," says Leonardo da Vinci. According to the kind of happiness he thirsts for, the greatness of a man can be recognized. The goods that attract a man and polarize his tensions also determine whether he is a personality in the true sense of the word. The greatness, depth and breadth of a man are revealed by the diminishing receptivity for all minor things which recede and even vanish before some major gift granted to him by God. Take the case of a man who beholds some new world of sublime transfigured beauty, as for instance in seeing Italy, the blessed land of redeemed beauty. If his interests in trivial goods, in familiar comforts, sports, amusements, is not immediately silenced and blunted, that man is a narrow individual. Again, a man receives the great gift of discovering another person who has a mysterious affinity with him; he fully understands the essential secret logos of that person and feels his own secret world understood by him so that they can become one in Jesus. Suppose that in spite of all this he does not spontaneously put aside and suppress his clinging to the familiar goods of life, is not inclined to sacrifice his "snugness," comfort and even his reputation as a reasonable man, which he enjoys in the eyes of his fellow citizens. If he is not ready to give up "all his possessions" and to consider them as naught, such a man is not a personality in the true sense of the word.

He alone is a true personality whose thirst for happiness cannot be satisfied with any created good, and who says with St. Augustine, "Our hearts are restless until they find their rest in Thee."

The criterion for determining whether a man is a true personality in the ultimate sense is found in his longing for God as the highest good, so that he cries "I have sought Thy face, O Lord (*Quaesivi vultum tuum, Domine*)"; in his inner awareness of that deepest level which God alone can fill; in his spontaneous readiness to subordinate and even, if necessary, to put aside all other ties to true goods when a ray from God's Face enters his soul, when the finger of God touches his soul; in his readiness to sell everything in order to acquire the unique pearl of the divine kingdom. This is the summit of all conformity to the objective gradation of values and goods for the person. Only he who possesses the right sense of this hierarchy and takes it into account in his joys and enthusiasms, in what he chooses and how he acts, in his desires and renunciations, in his receptivity and his attachments—only he possesses that spirit of inner freedom and breadth, unlimitedness, and dimension of greatness which characterizes true personality. Only he, moreover, is free from satiety and stagnation in blind alleys; only in him lives that longing to approach God ever closer which lends wings to man's whole being, discloses to him the knowledge of the cosmos, and, above all, leads him to seek and find in all values God's Face. This longing is a precondition for true communion with Christ and through Christ with the Holy Trinity. It is the longing of which St. Bonaventure speaks at the beginning of the *Itinerarium mentis in Deum*: ''These things can only be understood by him who, like Daniel, is a man of longing.''

In the Liturgy we find this *sense of the hierarchy of values* embodied in a unique fashion. The supreme, the absolutely primary place in our soul which it gives to God manifests this sense most expressly. The liturgical act itself means, to begin with, the putting in its rightful place of the only thing necessary (*unum necessarium*). In the early morning when the ''world'' is asleep, the glorification of God begins in Matins. This is not a hurried glance cast at God in a frame of mind already burdened with the tension of the day's work and the expectation of what the day may bring for us and our interests. It is a dwelling before God in a broad expansive rhythm, ''O Lord, Thou wilt open my lips: and my mouth shall declare Thy praise (*Domine, labia mea aperies et os meum annuntiabit laudem tuam*),'' a giving the first place to what is more important, to ''the work of God (*opus Dei*)'' which is urgent above all else, the praise and glorification of the only One ''from Whom are all things, by Whom are all things, in Whom are all things (*ex quo omnia, per quem omnia, in quo omnia sunt*).'' It is a contemplative lingering in the presence of the *magnalia Dei* and of the message of God addressed to us in the Lessons. After the Te Deum in which in praising, thanksgiving, and petitioning we traverse the entire content of revelation, a new stream of divine praise and glorification begins in Lauds; it is only in Prime that a glance is cast on the day which is beginning and the work it has in store for us, its joys and sorrows; then the day is placed before God with the prayer: ''Vouchsafe, O Lord, this day to keep us without sin (*Dignare, Domine, die isto sine peccato nos custodire*)''; ''And let the brightness of the Lord our God be upon us, and direct Thou the works of our hands over us; yea, the work of our hands do Thou direct (*Et sit splendor Domini Dei nostri super nos, et opera manuum nostrarum dirige super nos, et opus manuum nostrarum dirige*).''

The very breadth with which the Coram ipso, this ''standing before Him'' embedded in the prayer of Christ, is performed in preference to all other things is a clear manifestation of the truth of the Benedictine motto, ''Nothing must be placed before divine service (*Operi Dei nil praeponatur*).'' In this is expressed a classical formula for the clear awareness of the true hierarchy of values.

The perception of the true gradation of values is even more clearly expressed in the holy Sacrifice which we offer God through Christ, with Christ, and in Christ. Before all else must be offered to God the highest, the only adequate adoration and gift: His

87

only-begotten Son, Jesus Christ Himself. The one eternal Word which God has spoken and speaks eternally, which He has spoken to us in the Incarnation, we now are allowed to "speak" to Him, and then to receive Him, our resurrection and life. We can even now embrace the "longing of the eternal hills," and be mysteriously drawn into Him in Whom "the entire plenitude of Godhead is." Again and again during the day, we emerge from the stream of life and out of all that holds us in a state of movement and tension in order to turn to the eternally Same, to the unchanging, infinitely glorious and holy One, infinitely deserving of love. This rhythm of the Liturgy is the strongest expression of the true hierarchy of values.

In the articulation of the Liturgy also, and in the structure of the liturgical year, we find expressed in a unique fashion the spirit which demands that the true hierarchy of values be taken into account. The rank of each feast corresponds to the objective scale of its mystery, and this implies the inner melody which fills the entire Liturgy of the day, the degree of splendor, of joy, of glorification, the weight of commemoration, the entire display of festivity and jubilation.

All this is expressed vividly in the fact that certain parts of the Liturgy appear only in connection with a certain degree of festivity, such as the Credo in the Mass, the Te Deum in Matins, the Alleluia and its variations, a Sequence in the greatest feasts, and the proper Prefaces. Further, this spirit is reflected in the thought-content of the individual texts of various feasts as in the ''This is the day the Lord has made (*Haec dies quam fecit Dominus*)'' of Easter, and in the often repeated ''*Hodie*'' of Christmas. Again, we find this spirit in the atmosphere of the entire linguistic expression, the width and breadth of a feast's celebration, in its being preceded by a vigil in which its dawn is anticipated, and in its prolongation by an octave. And we also find it in the fact that all other feasts are displaced because of the greatness and splendor of the feast in question as expressed in the degree of ''exclusiveness'' of an octave; all this moreover is reflected in the modes of the plain chant, the celebration of high Mass with deacon and sub-deacon and incense and even in the outward decorations required by the feast, the display of candles, and so on. The hierarchy of values is also expressed in the fact that a secondary feast yields to the greater feast and makes way for it. It is the achievement of what we have defined above as the sign of true personality: the lesser value inwardly ''makes way'' for the greater value.

People who are not familiar with the spirit of the Liturgy think that this precise gradation of feasts, the exact regulations governing which feast takes precedence over another are but a form of juridical pedantry which should have no place in the religious sphere. But those who penetrate deeper will recognize that a great and central principle is here exemplified, a principle which should also influence the attitude toward the cosmos in the life of the individual, so that his life really be in tune with the objective logos of being.

VII

The Spirit of Awakenedness in the Liturgy

One of the deepest marks of true personality is the state of being spiritually awake. A genuine personality is distinguished from the average man precisely by the fact that he does not wade through life in a state of spiritual inertia; that he does not contemplate in an isolated way what approaches him, but beholds it in the light of the general cosmic background, *in conspectu Dei*, and lives in the metaphysical situation of man. This does not refer to an outward wakefulness, a certain alertness possessed by practical-minded people, and often found wanting in the spiritually gifted: a quick grasping and understanding of outward conditions, a certain preparedness and mental dexterity. This quality, so characteristic of practical people, may coincide with the absence of being inwardly awake that we here have in mind. On the other hand, this state of being inwardly awake is sometimes possessed to a high degree by people who are readily forgetful, who act distractedly, fail to grasp conditions and circumstances where practical business is concerned, lack a certain clearness, precision, and quickness of mind, and are therefore mocked by practical people and regarded as dreamers.

This state of being inwardly awake means turning our face spiritually toward the world of values, keeping ourselves open to their radiation; it means a preparedness to go along with them spiritually, to "conspire" with their meaning and content, to conform to the Sursum corda, the "let us lift up our hearts," which the values address to us, and to let ourselves be exalted by them. Many people are not blind to values, but they leave it to chance whether or not a value reveals itself and seizes them; they let themselves drift and be carried wherever the stream of circumstance directs their impulses and fleeting moods; they abandon themselves to the law of inertia in their nature; their life is a perpetual "letting oneself go," and hence a life on the periphery. They are spiritually asleep even when they are men of good character and good will. They allow themselves to be completely dominated by circumstances, and one day follows the other without their being "awakened" to a deeper insight into the world and themselves, without their questioning the meaning of things and themselves. Unquestioning, taking everything for granted, immersed in practical dealing and management, they live without ever experiencing "wonder" at being and its mysteries. However talented and gifted, such "unawake" men are not personalities. They do not really "live" their lives but let themselves, so to speak, "undergo" their lives.

There exist two dimensions of being awake. One is the attitude in which the depth of things is open to the person, an attitude of inner readiness to receive fully and to penetrate the essential that our spiritual eyes behold. The other is the awareness of the entire metaphysical frame in all that one experiences, the consideration of all things against this background and ultimately in the light of God; it is the bearing deeply in mind of the fundamental truths once grasped, and, above all, the truth of the metaphysical situation of man. The roots of these two dimensions are intertwined and represent two manifestations of the one fundamental attitude of being awake. In certain persons, one of these ways may be more developed that the other. Yet both dimensions belong to true personality.

In this sphere there are different *degrees* of the state of being awake to the true nature of the world. The first degree is the general inclination toward the realm of values and their meaning. This distinguishes the "awake" from the obtuse man. Obtuse people ignore the deep content of all the spheres of life, they see only the obvious which needs no spiritual *élan* in order to be grasped; when they grasp a value, they hold it at a "reasonable distance," without letting their hearts be inflamed by its glow. The man who, on the contrary, possesses the first degree of being "awake" enters into relations with many spheres of life, the beauty of nature and art, the earnestness and dignity of knowledge, the charm of the world of vital values; and the relationship may be a very intensive one. Life in its many-colored and multiform aspects speaks loudly and clearly to him. He lives a full life in a state of openness, readiness and deep spiritual receptiveness. According to the depth of his gifts, this man's state of being awake may present various dimensions until it reaches that of a great genius.

A second degree is the state of being awake to moral consciousness: the understanding of the inflexible earnestness of the demands of the sphere of moral values, which address themselves to us without asking us what pleases us; the shining forth of the metaphysical situation of man, the discovery of our own power to say to all that arises before us a free "yes" or "no" according to whether or not it is an objective value. A man may possess a certain awakenedness regarding many spheres of life and being, and yet not have reached moral maturity and consciousness. Supported by great gifts and talents, he may resist a spiritual inertia and be ready to follow the values spiritually; the surrounding world may also speak to him in strong and direct language; free from all conventional desubstantialization, he may be aware of the colorful originality and full-blooded content of things; his life may be full of intensity and inner content. Yet such a man may not be awake to the understanding of the world of values in its majesty and intrinsic dignity. He has not yet grasped the fact that a response is "due" to values; he has not yet understood that the domain of values is beyond our pleasure and the fortuitous inclinations of our nature. He has not yet discovered his own freedom, that freedom which allows us to rise above the inclinations of our nature, to follow the lead of values and turn away from nonvalues independently of the whims of our temperament; the freedom which grants us the possibility of sanctioning or disavowing our impulses, accepting or refusing an offer made by life. An entirely new and decisive degree of awakenedness is implied in this moral consciousness which awakens a man to a fundamentally new understanding of the sphere of values and makes him find "himself" and his own freedom; which allows him to grasp the fact that only the conscious, expressly sanctioned response-to-value satisfies the demand of the realm of values.

As one easily perceives, this moral maturity is an indispensable foundation of true personality. Without it a man remains infantile in the center of his being, and never ripens into spiritual maturity. In spite of its fullness and vitality, a man's life without this maturity is plunged in "slumber," in the deeper sense of the word.

A third degree of being awake is the inner openness to God, the harkening to God's voice and to the call of God. This religious awakenedness means the inner readiness to commit oneself to the world of

Liturgy and Personality

God's mysteries, the state of "keeping oneself open" to the world of God hidden from our natural sight, the state of the patriarchs of the Old Testament, for example, which is also found in St. John the Baptist, in the apostles and disciples who followed the call of Christ, and in all who have "ears to hear" when God speaks.

This deepest form of awakenedness, this opening of the deepest spiritual "organ" for the reception of God's voice, indirectly in creation and directly in His supernatural revelation, is more than the precondition of faith. It continues also into the very life of the faith where, transfigured now by grace, it is an essential element of the true relationship with God even for him who has found God and is supernaturally bound to Him through Christ and His Church. It is the foundation for a deeper penetration into the truth of faith, for a deeper irradiation by the light in our souls, grasping for the invitation of grace in us, for true prayer, and for inner cooperation with Christ when the Holy Ghost acts mysteriously in us. This is the degree of awakenedness which alone makes of man a true personality, for it is both an indispensable precondition within us for the transformation into Christ and, at the same time, part of the resemblance to Christ. There are people who, though fortunate enough to possess faith, are yet not awake: spiritually and mentally inert people, who lack the necessary inner readiness and tension, and live in a relative obtuseness. Their being cannot be truly transformed by the supernatural. They have not opened their depths

96

in order to let the life of grace stream into them; they keep the supernatural life bestowed upon them by baptism "bottled up" in themselves.

True awakenedness implies receptiveness to God's voice; it implies an inner readiness for the Lord and a knowledge of ourselves. "Who art thou and who am I?" Such is the question of the person who is awake. *"Noverim te, noverim me* (Could I but know Thee, could I but know myself)"; such is the longing cry of one who is awake. It implies the grasping of the true situation of our own self before God; the confrontation, previously described, of our own self with God. It is an inner self-opening, allowing oneself to be irradiated by the light of God in order to know and find oneself in this light.

Here we find the two dimensions of awakenedness previously mentioned. We find this ultimate letting-oneself-remain-open, this readiness and receptiveness spoken of by Christ in the Parable of the Wise and Foolish Virgins, in the vigil of the Advent of the Lord, of which we know "neither the day, nor the hour." This vigil forbids us to live at our leisure, to let ourselves go peripherally along with the impulses of our fallen nature in such a way that our ears become obdurate and no longer hear what God says to us, and we "slumber" when the Lord calls us. But we also find the other dimension—the life *in conspectu Dei*, constantly keeping in mind the true situation in which we live. This awakenedness forbids us to be so absorbed by certain goods as to forget God, the "first truth"; it prevents us from living so intensely in the visible world which surrounds us as to forget what stands behind and above that world, in the light of which alone all that belongs to the visible world acquires its genuine visage. It is the awakenedness in which we do not allow ourselves to be absorbed by what is at hand, by urgent business and the day's work, but rather keep ourselves centered on God and His kingdom, on our vocation and the supernatural meaning of our lives. In a word, it is the awakenedness which is a dwelling in the presence of God, an abiding in His light. Both dimensions are interlinked. The more we live with our gaze fixed on God, abide in the consciousness of that only true world and of our own fundamental situation, and see everything in that light—and the more open we are and receptive—the more does the deep content of all that falls under our spiritual eyes speak to us and the more acute is our ear for hearing the voice of God. From this awakenedness organically flows also the knowlege of the dangers threatening our ultimate vocation, and the need to watch over temptations. This awareness of dangers, however, does not constitute the entire content of true awakenedness, but is merely part of it.

It is to both these forms of being awake that the Lord urges us with extraordinary force in the Gospels: "Watch ye therefore, because you know not the day nor the hour when the Lord cometh"; "Behold, watch and pray!"; "And what I say to you, I say to all: watch!"; "Be you then also ready"; "Watch ye, and pray that ye will not enter into temptation."

Awakenedness in the Liturgy

There are few attitudes to which the Lord urges us with so much insistence as to that of awakenedness. The apostles do likewise: "But be thou vigilant"; and, "Let us not sleep as others do, but let us watch," says St. Paul; "Be prudent therefore, and watch in prayers," says St. Peter; "Blessed is he that watcheth," says St. John in the Apocalypse.

The Liturgy is pervaded with this spirit of awakenedness. The Liturgy is a vigil in itself in the highest sense of the word and organically draws all who live in it into this spirit. In liturgical prayer, we emerge from the grip of our interests and worries, the tensions centered on our labors, the immediate goals of practical life, the importunate beckoning by isolated sections of the visible and tangible world around us; we emerge toward the great things that are eternally and invariably important, toward the *mysterium Divinitatis*, the *mysterium Trinitatis*, the *mysterium Incarnationis*, the *mysterium misericordiae et caritatis*, the *magnalia Dei*, the great deeds of God, the mystery of the Suffering Christ and the Eucharist. We emerge from the visible, not just to cast a fleeting glance on that world of mysteries, but to abide in it at length, believing, hoping, loving, thanking, praying, asking. All this is the *expressed accomplishment* of awakenedness. We sacrifice and pray during the Hours of the day, not in order to become awake, but in order to glorify God. Yet this deep, broad stream of liturgical prayer before God is the actualization of being awake. Participation in the prayer of Christ means to be awake in the highest sense of the word. The performing of the Liturgy means also being awake to ourselves and our true metaphysical situation. Thanks to the Liturgy, we stand consciously where we objectively stand in truth. Here the cardboard houses of pride collapse; all the illusions of concupiscence, all repression, all flight from God and from oneself, all the self-beguilement which is implied in turning away from true reality; all of this falls to pieces. Our sin, our guilt, our responsibility, death—which none of us can escape—the danger of eternal damnation, our nothingness before God, God's infinite mercy, our redemption through the blood of Christ—all stand revealed before us. In the Liturgy which we perform through, with, and in Christ, Who is eternal truth, we are *placed into truth*. All semblance and twilight are dispelled through the *lumen Christi*; all is laid bare in that light—ourselves, our condition, our vocation.

All earthly goods, our earthly actions and designs, are also set in their right place, *in conspectu Dei*. To be awake is not only extended to eternal things, but also to transient and earthly ones. The Liturgy is in itself awakenedness in the highest sense of the word; and it leads, moreover, all who live in it to this same state.

Throughout the course of the day with its Hours, through a continually renewed "treading before God," the man threatened with being drawn into the turmoil of life is again lifted upward toward awakenedness. Where do we recognize more deeply the consequence of original sin than in our bluntness and thoughtlessness? We know that inasmuch as we are baptized, the life of Christ pulsates in us, that the Most Holy Trinity dwells in us, but how often in the course of the day do we live in that consciousness? We know that Christ stands before us in our neighbor, but how many people do we actually behold in that light? We know that "only one thing is necessary," but we trouble about many things. When a ray of God's glory touches our soul and our heart is filled to overflowing, how long does this condition last before we drop back into the periphery and are absorbed by trifles? God may grant us a great gift, He may let us discover a human being whom we understand ultimately and who likewise understands us, a human being whom we may love with Jesus and in Jesus, in whom we may grasp the unduplicable design of God which he represents, toward whom we have an ultimate mission, and who has an ultimate mission toward us. Yet how soon do we grow accustomed to this gift, how soon does God's kindness become something habitual in our eyes, how soon, in our inertia, do we grow deaf to the call of God implied in the gift, and let it be drowned out in the whirlpool of the commonplace? What bluntness in marriage, in friendship, in our relations with children! What bluntness toward all the goods, of every kind, which God's bounty bestows on us, whether it be the beauty of nature, the splendor of truth, and health, or of liberty! For how much of all this do we thank God? How soon does that for which we longed, as for something rare and precious, grow commonplace in our eyes!

Liturgy and Personality

We can measure our bluntness by comparison with the *Confessions* of a St. Augustine or by contemplating a St. Francis of Assisi. In these we find true awakenedness, the victory over all routine and bluntness, a beholding of all things in *conspectu Dei*, a harkening to the voice of God which speaks to us in all goods and providential gifts! Here is a true perception of God's most generous bounty, His inebriating sweetness, a true grasping of all things in their original significance which embodies God's creative design for them. The Liturgy leads us to this condition of being fully awake by withdrawing us from the daily process of becoming blunted; it lifts us out of spiritual slumber, the obtuse "taking all goods for granted," being dazzled by the new only because it is new. The Liturgy frees us from all this by inviting us to emerge at certain intervals of the day into the light of God and to actualize our awakenedness in the endless stream of praise, thanksgiving and prayer. But one might ask: Is the Liturgy the only path to this awakening? Do not the many brief glances we lift to God in the course of the day, marking thus our perception of our true situation, bring about this same awakenedness? Is it not enough, before each task, joy or sorrow, to perform an act of good intention and link all to God?

Without underrating the value of the brief upward glance and good intention, it must nevertheless be said that they can never replace the formation in awakenedness granted by the Liturgy. First of all, they lack the organic character of the latter. The

Liturgy, as has been previously pointed out, is not performed in order to become awake, but only because we owe God adoration, glorification, and thanksgiving, and because we must ask Him to grant us what we need for our salvation. It is not a means for becoming awake; indeed it is itself the highest form of being awake. In this lies, as we have already seen, the highest and most organic mode of inner transformation; we become awake *in* the Liturgy, not *through* the Liturgy. Furthermore, the Liturgy does not consist in arbitrary glances lifted upward at certain moments of the day; it is organically linked with the rhythm of the day, with the situation in which each of us is placed independently of his choosing. Finally, it is not a mere rapid glance but a prolonged "abiding" before God, a "standing before Him" for a long while. It is not a rigid, momentary act of emerging, but an organic unfolding before God. The peaceful rhythm of contemplation and the granting to ourselves of all the necessary time that inhere in the Liturgy lead us along quite a different path into the world of God, liberate us far more organically and efficaciously from the tensions caused by the earthly rhythm of everyday business.

The meaning of the upward glance is certainly an emerging from tensions; through it we should cease to cling to immediate aims, to what must be "accomplished directly," and enter into the presence of that which is alone important, the eternally essential. It should be a brief eruption of the contemplative attitude in the face of the practical. But these brief upward glances too often also become a "means" which we use hurriedly, still absorbed by the cramped attitude of practical life, and only in order to be able to return with an eased conscience to the turmoil of work. The brief upward glances are not superfluous. They are necessary and even indispensable for the state of being awake. But they cannot replace what is implied here by the Liturgy. They are in their right place only against the background of the Liturgy and growing out of it organically.

Secondly, and this is even more important, liturgical prayer means emerging from the narrowness of one's own life and rejoining the life of Christ and the universal sphere of the praying Church. It is an immersion into the world of God. The man who is bound only to God by brief upward glances and good intentions remains fixed in his own life; he moves in a religious atmosphere which corresponds to his own subjective narrowness; he lives on an image of God and Christ which he has formed by himself. Often, for him, God plays the part of a formidable ruler dominating his life, to whom he must pray to obtain what he longs for, to whom he formally links everything, to whom he must after all offer up everything; but He is a God in Whose presence one does not linger, Whose rays do not irradiate one, to Whom one does not give oneself up in pure response-to-value. Such men may also be pious and full of good will; for them too, God is a final end; but they draw God into *their* lives and see Him through the glasses of their own narrowness; they have lost the sense of true proportion; the air they breathe daily is too much determined by the narrow scope of their particular lives, even though they might be embellished with religion. Such men do not actually emerge from their lives in order to meet God; the fundamental rhythm of their existence is not immersion in God's world and the *magnalia Dei*, nor a participation in the adoring and sacrificing love of Christ; they do not let their lives flow into the life of Christ. This danger cannot be sufficiently stressed!

Emergence from the narrowness of our life and "awakening" to the true world of God are such difficult tasks for our fallen nature, even after its restoration through membership in the Mystical Body of Christ, that the simple good intention and the brief upward glance do not suffice to overcome the difficulties. This latter form of relationship depends on the peculiar capacity of the person, while in the Liturgy we enter into a relationship molded by God. The fundamental attitude and thought-content of the Liturgy, its form and entire qualitative atmosphere, breathe the spirit of Christ; they plunge us therefore into being awake to the true world of the supernatural.

Here again the merit of good intention should not be minimized; it has its significance, but it cannot replace the Liturgy as the path to the state of being genuinely awake. As long as the day is filled with good intentions only, the danger mentioned above is not excluded; furthermore, only the person formed by the Liturgy will be able to realize the good intentions in the right way. Only in the latter case will the intention receive its authentic molding. Of course, God can bestow awakenedness on the man who does not observe the Hours or attend daily Mass. But we do not speak here of what God may bestow through extraordinary graces; we speak of what He has bestowed in the Liturgy.

The Liturgy, both in its entirety and in its individual parts, is a world of full ''vigilance'' in the highest sense of the word. This awakenedness is actualized pre-eminently in the holy Sacrifice of the Mass, through which we are drawn into the full reality of the sacrifice on the cross, and into the God-man's act of adoring and atoning love.

Furthermore, in its very structure the Liturgy is a being awake and a being awakened. The frequent repetition of the Credo represents a particular form of ''vigilance.'' We affirm our belief in the entire content of revelation as a response owed to God. We expressly render account to the supernatural reality in renewed professions of faith. This carries with it the achievement of being awake to the reality of the supernatural. Again and again, the latter arises before our spiritual eyes, so easily distracted by the visible world. It is the same with the continually repeated Gloria Patri, and the Te Deum of the Matins of feasts; every morning the great call resounds, ''Today, if you shall hear his voice, harden not your hearts (*Hodie, si vocem ejus audieritis, nolite obdurare corda vestra*).'' Even the participation of the body in religious worship, as in the act of genuflection, the inclination of the head during the Gloria, and the standing during the reading of the Gospels, represents an attitude of awakenedness, and at the same time a call to wakefulness. What a confirmation of the full reality of the supernatural is disclosed in the fact that, even in our physical deportment, we conduct ourselves toward what is before us as though it stood visibly in front of our eyes! This deportment, which may appear to many as a mere outward gesture, is a deep expression of full awakenedness in which we touch supernatural reality. It draws us into the full genuine "standing face to face." It is an expression of inner readiness, a "standing before God" which helps us to awaken from bluntness, inertia, the shutting up of oneself in oneself.

What a deep and noble symbol of watchfulness is revealed in the praise of God in the night when the world "sleeps," in the Matins, and formerly in all the vigils. Here the "vigil" even becomes an actual theme; as opposed to the sleeping world, this soaring upward to the true reality is expressed in a peculiarly vivid fashion, as in the hymn of Tuesday's Matins:

> O God from God, and light from light,
> Who art Thyself the day.
> Our chants shall break the clouds of night,
> Be with us while we pray.
>
> Chase the sloth and drowsiness that bind
> The senses with a spell.*

> *Consors paterni luminis,
> Lux ipse lucis et dies,
> Noctem canendo rumpimus:
> Assiste postulantibus.*
>
> *Expelle somnolentiam,
> Ne pigritantes obruat.*

Liturgy and Personality

The unfolding of the liturgical year as a whole is also an expression of awakenedness and vigilance. Here we find repeated on a larger scale what the liturgical day represents on a smaller one. We watch before God by keeping in mind the great fact of salvation—full of unchanging significance—as well as the *magnalia Dei*, and by participating in the sublime rhythm of the liturgical year. The liturgical days do not concern themselves with the crowding events in the limited daily lives of individuals or communities or states; they are wholly preoccupied with the consciousness of the *magnalia Dei*. The great deeds of God determine the days and the sections of time in the Liturgy. What a state of wakefulness is implied by this! This is indeed a victorious drive, a breaking through all the strata of earthly events clustering around us, the misery of individuals and peoples, the entanglements of states and families, as well as the temporal destiny of the Church. It is a drive toward *supernatural* reality.

Moreover, how organic is this form of being awake! During Advent, the Church invites us to participate in the longing of thousands of years, and awakens us in order to await the Advent of the Lord: ''Brothers, knowing the season, that it is now the hour for us to arise from sleep . . . ,'' the holy Church calls to us at the beginning of Advent. The Gospel of the First Sunday of Advent places the return of Christ clearly before our eyes. The longing is a specific expression of awakenedness. The worst form of slumbering, of bluntness, is to be so absorbed in our business of life that we do not even long for God any more. The entirely blunted man is the satiated one, the man who, satisfied with himself and the world, does not ask for anything beyond.

Advent is followed by Christmas and the Epiphany. What a call to awaken we hear each year at this time, as if the event were happening today, as if we were hearing the message for the first time! What a call to awaken resounds in the rejoicing over the birth of our Lord: the continually repeated *"Hodie"* of Christmas; the praise and thanksgiving offered to God for the Incarnation of the eternal Word in the "Behold the Lord the Ruler is come! (*Ecce advenit Dominator Dominus*)," and in the "Arise, be enlightened, O Jerusalem: for thy light is come, and the glory of the Lord is risen upon thee! (*Surge, illuminare, Jerusalem, quia venit lumen tuum, et gloria Domini super te orta est*)," and in the "We have seen his star in the east (*Vidimus stellam ejus in Oriente*)" of the Epiphany. Then comes the time of Lent. It is the time of the great placing of ourselves in a confrontation with God, the full awakening to our burden of guilt and the necessity of atonement and penance before God. We are led into that aspect of awakening which is called self-knowledge, the seeing of ourselves in the light of God; and at the same time we are introduced to the mercy of God which offers us the possibility of penance, atonement, and reconciliation in Christ and through Christ. *"Ecce nunc tempus acceptabile, ecce nunc dies salutis* (Behold now is the acceptable time, behold now is the day of salvation)," the Church sings on the First Sunday of Lent. Then comes Passion Week in which we awaken to the mystery of Christ's suffering; Holy Week in which we are immersed in the mystery of the Eucharist and the death on the cross; and then the feast of all feasts, the great awakening to the light of the Resurrection, the glory of the Resurrected, the new opening of the doors of eternity through victory over death: "O Death, where is thy sting?" The culminating point of all awakenedness is Easter and the time of Easter: "Seek the things that are above, where Christ is sitting at the right hand of God; taste the things that are above, not the things that are upon the earth (*Quae sursum sunt quaerite, ubi Christus est in dextera Dei sedens; quae sursum sunt sapite, non quae super terram*)." These words of the Vigil Mass at Easter are the quintessence of awakenedness. This time is followed by the Ascension and the nine days of "awaiting" the Holy Ghost. Where do we find a more deeply expressed unfolding of awakenedness in the sense of inner preparedness and harkening than in these nine days which we spend with the apostles in the Upper Room? Then comes Pentecost and we awake anew to the mystery of the descent of the Holy Ghost.

Here the state of awakenedness expressed in the liturgical year and its sublime rhythm can be grasped. In the liturgical cycle, the Church irradiates our life with the world of the supernatural; it draws us into the cycle of the mysteries of faith; we breathe the fragrance of Christ; we hear His voice; we live His life. And this is not a haphazard meditation on the mysteries of faith in which we merely indulge in an artificial act of an intellectual or emotional nature; it is an organic participation in the pulse of the entire Church, a breathing with the Church, a life in the Church. Each day is marked and shaped by the Liturgy in such a fashion that it draws us of itself into the supernatural reality so that we live our life surrounded by it on all sides. Each day is so deeply penetrated with this "watch" before God in sacrifice, praise and thanksgiving that we naturally grow more and more awake. The Liturgy, as has been already often stressed, is the deepest form of awakenedness because its aim is not to awaken us but to give the adequate answer to God's majesty and holiness.

The man formed by the Liturgy is the man who is awake in the highest sense of the word. He is not only inwardly open to hearing the voice of God; he is not only aware of the ultimate Truth, but he also looks on all earthly goods in their true light. Far removed from all bluntness, "indifference," stoic insensibility and impassiveness, his awakened ear is open to every created thing in its mysterious message from above, in its God-given meaning. His heart is open to the precious and noble character of created things, such as water, for instance, as disclosed in the blessing of the baptismal water. What a contrast to all the blunt, obvious conceptions of earthly goods received from God's paternal hand is found in the liturgical "Benedicite"! What constantly awakened gratitude!—"The eyes of all wait upon Thee, O Lord, and Thou givest them their meat in due season (*Oculi omnium in te sperant, Domine, et tu das escam illorum in tempore opportuno*)." "Bless us, O Lord, and these Thy gifts which we are about to receive from Thy bounty (*Benedic, Domine, nos et haec tua dona, quae de tua largitate sumus sumpturi*)." "We give Thee thanks, O almighty God, for all Thy mercies (*Agimus tibi gratias omnipotens Deus, pro universis beneficiis tuis*)." At the same time, everything is organically placed into relation with the supernatural so that our spirit can rejoin again and again the unique and eternal, the goal of our hope: "May the King of eternal glory make us participate in the divine banquet (*Mensae caelestis participes faciat nos Rex aeternae gloriae*)."

The man formed by the Liturgy watches, so to speak, with a "burning lamp in his hand," and "with girt loins," for the advent of the Lord. His life is a life of longing, hope, gratitude, solemn emotion, and openness to the mysteries of being. We see how deeply awakenedness is linked with reverence, as well as with the consciousness that an adequate response is due to value, and with the sense of the right gradation of values. The awakened man is also conscious of the ultimate tie which binds him to all men before God; he sees Christ in his neighbor; he lives in the truth of the Mystical Body of Christ. To the extent that a man is awakened in this sense, he exists fully as a person, he genuinely *lives*, his life is true, he is a personality in the original sense of the word.

It is particularly important today to stress this point. In a legitimate reaction against an analytical, self-reflective consciousness, many have fallen into the cult of a naive unconsciousness, a childish un-awakenedness. This is a falling into Charybdis in order to avoid Scylla. A wrong self-consciousness is of course disastrous, whether it takes the form of a "squinting" at the accomplishment of our life, in a *curious* looking backward at our actions and attitudes just in the living moment instead of focusing on the object, or whether it takes the form of an intellectual analysis and dissection of the world and ourselves in which we no longer see the woods for the trees. In either case, it is a hypertrophy of the analytical attitude which leaves no room for a contemplative possession of an object. But the unconscious man also is incomplete; he is an unauthentic half-man. True consciousness, an indispensable element of personality and an essential part of the transformation into Christ, is nothing but awakenedness. It means emerging from all the mists of the "vital" and the "unconscious" into the brightness of the logos; it means being irradiated by the *lumen Christi*. It also means the ripening toward that full awakenedness which we shall actually possess only in eternity when we shall be flooded by the *lumen gloriae*; when we no longer see through a glass in an obscure manner, but face to face; when we no longer know in part, but as we have been known. The great motto of this earthly life must be, "Watch ye therefore, because you know not the day nor the hour."

VIII

The Spirit of 'Discretio' in the Liturgy

Closely linked with the state of being awake and with the spirit of the hierarchy of values, there exists a certain *discretio*. It is the sense of distinguishing as applied to the world-structure. In the first place, it is a specific sense for the structure and the dramatic rhythm of being, of preparation, ascension, fulfillment, and decline. It is a sense for the stages of the inner development of a given theme, until we reach the "now" of its fulfillment. This dramatic rhythm —encountered not only in the course of the day with its morning, noon and evening, or in the cycle of the seasons, or in life with its youth, maturity and old age, but also repeated in many particular situations of life—does not always have the same form of rise, culminating point and descent. More precisely, in the highest and most central spheres of being, as for

Liturgy and Personality

instance in all that concerns the preparation for eternity, this rhythm is an ascension toward an everlasting summit. This rhythm is found in the conversion of a man, leading him to become a member of the Mystical Body of Christ and reaching its climax in holiness, never to decline. That which unfolds itself in time implies an inner dramatic character, an inner organic rhythm of development. Everything requires its own time of inner ripening in order to be genuine and true. The sense of the law of the inner development of all things, which varies according to the sphere of being, is an element of that *discretio*, of that discrimination, which is a mark of personality.

The fading of this sense is one of the most serious signs of the decay of the nineteenth and twentieth centuries. It is closely related to the technicalization, instrumentalization, and leveling of our world. In the eyes of a great number of people, the mechanical world of technique has become the model for all vital situations and all spheres of being. Men want to reach their goal as soon as possible, and "by the shortest way"—as it is reached in building a machine. They want to leave aside all the so-called "superfluous bywork." This activist, irreverent attitude results in the dying out of the rhythmical law of the being's inner unfolding, especially in the vital, intellectual and spiritual spheres. Men have ceased to understand what an indispensable function the superfluous so-called "bywork" possesses; they have ceased to conspire with the objective logos of things;

they want to fabricate things brutally, from the outside, without any sense of the dramatic character of the being's unfolding itself in time. They continually make short cuts.

That man who is indiscriminate in the sense described above understands nothing of the inner structure of a relationship of communion, especially of a communion of love, such as friendship or marriage. He does not understand the inner stages which must be traversed organically in the formation of an "I-thou-communion"; he does not understand that an inner law must be observed in progressing along the path leading from a reserved attitude toward another person to loving interpenetration. He does not realize the arrival of the moment which marks the passing from the more general "you" to the more intimate "thou"; he does not let himself be guided by the objective logos of the relationship, but blindly seeks to skip all the inner degrees of the formation of a deep relationship. But he skips them only in imagination, for in reality they cannot be skipped. He will never come to that which can only reached after traversing these stages—a deep "I-thou" communion. This does not mean that the mounting of objectively-presented degrees always requires the same amount of time for everyone. Sometimes the progress is slow; sometimes it is rapid; sometimes it is instantly achieved, according to the special character of the persons involved and their objective affinity to each other. But the stages must be objectively *passed through* and cannot be skipped. Indiscriminate persons disclose the innermost secrets of their hearts; they say ''thou''; they behave as if a deep ''I-thou'' communion already existed; they are not aware that they are still objectively in the peripheral position of an ''outside contact'' with the other person. Such people do not suspect that for every inner ''word'' filled with deep meaning, there exists a ''fullness of time'' in which alone it can be validly spoken.

Such are the people, too, who believe that one can ''establish'' a religious order provided one has in mind an adequate religious aim, just as one creates a religious association. They think that a suitable plan and a meritorious aim are also sufficient here in order to call a sacred entity into being. They believe it is quite possible to start a propaganda campaign in favor of their plan, with the aid of books and speeches, and thus to recruit the members of the future community. They do not understand that such a sacred entity must grow silently from within. The founder must not only conceive a good idea but must, above all, lead a life dedicated to God. Without planning the creation of a religious order, he simply obeys God's call in leading a life according to evangelical counsel. Then others will crystallize around him and form a life which will later be firmly shaped from within; this was the case with the Benedictine, Franciscan and Jesuit orders.

Equally, men lacking the spirit of *discretio* do not realize the stages of listening, receiving, quietude, recollection and silence, which must be observed before an explicit apostolate becomes possible. There are people who immediately after conversion, and as soon as they have found their way into the sanctuary, want to act apostolically and redress wrongs instantly. They do not feel how much time is required for listening, silence, prayer, and inner preparation by God, in order that an apostolate may be validly filled with the life of grace, and yield its fruit in the Lord's vineyard. Here we find the same defective sense of the inner dramatic essence of being, the same incomprehension of the inner stages which must be traversed before the moment has come to speak the inner word genuinely.

The fading of the sense of *discretio*, which we witness today, is expressed in the smallest things. Many consider that it is a superfluous convention to welcome one's friends expressly before speaking of other things, or to take leave of them; so, too, when it comes to saying ''good morning'' and ''good night'' to persons who share one's home. They do not grasp the fact that this custom implies a deep meaning—the necessity for conforming to the inner demands of a communion-situation. The fact of being together with other men demands objectively that before casting a common glance at the material, before exchanging impressions and experiences, there should be accomplished an act expressly meant for the other person as such, in which the ''bi-personal range'' is established. It is the same with every leave-taking. To skip and neglect these things is a violence done to the

Liturgy and Personality

inner structure of every communion-situation. The uttered welcome and farewell imply not only an expression of outward courtesy as does, for instance, the conventional use of a title, but they also imply a far deeper dimension. They imply the fact of taking the other human being seriously, of giving him full consideration as a person; they mean that one fully takes into account the interpersonal situation and its organic structure. To skip and overlook this fact, as if it were a superfluous formality, to regard it as fussy and ceremonious are typical cases of the lack of *discretio.*

Along with this incomprehension, we find the lack of a sense for the inner fullness and scope of certain moments, of the full ''now'' in which an inner development reaches its culminating point and in which something prodigious attains completion. It is the lack of the sense for these moments in our life which may be compared to what in the evolution of the world are called ''historical moments.'' In the eyes of indiscriminate persons, life flows so uniformly that they do not grasp the inner solemnity of a moment charged with meaning; for them, there is no full ''now.'' They have no feeling for the decisive, solemn ''now'' of such a moment as when a bridge is suddenly established between themselves and another person through a first loving glance. They have no feeling for the ''now'' of a farewell before a long separation, or a meeting after a long absence; nor do they feel the ''now'' of a man's birth and death, the ''now'' of baptism and conversion, a deep breakthrough or a great decision. With what a deep symbolism were all important moments, in which a new phase of life was to begin, formerly clothed, with a symbolism which stressed the decisive character of the event! Suffice it to recall the ceremonies held when a person was knighted, promoted from the state of apprentice to that of master, received a doctor's degree, or signed a contract.

Compare these cermonies to the way contracts are signed even by nations in the present, not to speak of the casual passing from one professional degree to another. What a leveling of all solemn moments! Is this not a clear sign of the fading of the sense of the full ''now''?

The spirit of *discretio* implies secondly a sense for the strata of depth at which one moves and should move, not mixing up the levels and not passing unaware from one level to the other. Many people, finding themselves in a certain situation, glide from a genuinely religious attitude into the far more peripheral one of a simple profession of their *own* convictions, without even noticing this transition. How many slip from a reverent attitude of obedience to God into the sphere of merely correct allegiance and propriety! They slip from the sphere of sincere sorrow into that of self-pity. They mix up the superficial emotions caused by childhood memories with true religious emotion. They pass from the deep stratum of self-donation to a person in need to the merely sporting enjoyment of being useful. There are women who pass from the sphere of loving-sacrifice to that of the mere satisfation of their motherly instincts. Though a woman's care for her husband may have been in the beginning an expression of devoted love, it may become imperceptibly a feeling of self-satisfaction brought on by taking care of someone, or it may even become an occasion for displaying domestic talents. It is not the satisfaction as such which is detrimental to *discretio*, but the fact of not noticing that it is something superficial compared to the genuine, initial, loving-sacrifice. There are men who, without being aware of it, pass from the sphere of genuine asceticism into that of a self-discipline akin to the training required by athletics. Others abandon genuine apostolic activity for the task of recruiting members to the "cause" of their own party.

It is a sign of true personality to distinguish the various levels of depth in oneself and not slip unaware from the depth to the surface in one's attitude toward a given good. Yes, a true personality has such a sense of the different levels in himself that he approaches a good only at the depth suitable to it; he is incapable of speaking of deep things while preserving a peripheral attitude; he feels the inner impossibility of shifting onto the peripheral plane those things which belong to the depths. The indiscriminate man, in this sense of the word, will also fail to distinguish the various strata in other persons; he will say things at the wrong moment; he will crudely lay bare and force to the surface things lying in the depths of the other persons. Such men desubstantialize many things by speaking in the wrong way about them, by repeating peripherally things that were genuinely spoken in the depths. When they are entrusted with the innermost secrets of another, they do not receive this ''word'' in their own corresponding depth, but let it drop into the periphery of mere loquacity.

One must not, however, interpret *discretio* as an appanage of reserved men, as if the uttering of what lies in the depths were already detrimental to *discretio*, and as if expansive people were always indiscreet. The question is not whether a person is reserved or expansive, but whether or not, in them, the level of expression and divulgence of an experience corresponds to the depths of the experience. Men who relate their most intimate affairs to everyone, who confide deep things to insensitive and uncomprehending people, are indiscriminate in our sense of the word. An adequate divulgence, however, an opening of oneself in a corresponding situation, is precisely a sign of *discretio*. For it also implies the utterance of the ''word'' objectively demanded at the given moment, instead of leaving it in the darkness of silence. The discriminate, in our sense of the word, understand precisely the necessity of divulging exactly at the right moment what is then thematic.

Finally, this *discretio* implies a sense for the different gradations which may exist in our relations to, or connections with, a certain good, especially the kingdom of God. This sense is possessed naturally by most people in respect to certain spheres. Take, for instance, the building of a palace, let us say the Palazzo Farnese in Rome, upon which many artisans and workmen as well as great artists like Sangallo and Michelangelo were employed. The gradation in their various relations to the essential theme—the realization of a work of art—should be apparent to everyone, except the hopelessly obtuse. It is obvious that the activity of the artist is penetrated with the objective logos of the work of art, while the work of the mason is only superficially in contact with its spirit. The activity of the mason is not in itself qualitatively stamped with the logos of the work in question, so that it can be distinguished essentially from the masonry in the building of an inferior, artistically defective monument. In the building of the Farnese Palace, it is true, this activity bears quite a different value because it serves something beautiful; while in the case of an artistically defective monument, it represents a negative value, not in the moral sense of course, but insofar as it contributes to the creation of something ugly. It is, of course, desirable for the mason to possess artistic understanding and rejoice in his participation in the creation of beauty. His work will then acquire subjectively a new quality through the consciousness of serving a value, and this consciousness will render it more noble. But this does not alter the fact that this form of service to the objective value is far more loosely linked to the good. And the mason must humbly admit that the artist's service is bound to the value by a far deeper and more significant link.

As we have said above, here the gradation is clearly seen by almost anyone. In certain other spheres, however, especially in the religious one, many have

lost the sense of gradation in the service of the kingdom of God. Of course, all that we do should be subjectively transformed into service to God. But the
objective distinctions which consist in the *kind* of service rendered to the kingdom of God should not be
effaced. We must possess the clear sense of how far a
service, useful in itself to the reign of God, is objectively
stamped with its seal, how far it is sacred, how much it
approaches the original theme of the reign of God.

Many people have ceased to be aware of the difference in degree of service between the organizing of
a political party founded on Catholic principles and
an apostolate in behalf of the kingdom of God based
on preaching and example. Many people believe that
the recruiting of members for a Catholic association
has the same rank as the preaching of a homily. There
are many instances in which, for example, a pious
Catholic is a distinguished scholar in some neutral
scientific sphere, and thus, by his activity, gives evi-
dence that there is no contradiction between scientific
research and the Catholic faith. His scientific activity
thus serves indirectly the kingdom of God. Many will
place this action on the same scale as that of an
apostolate expressed in life-long scholarly work inwardly penetrated and fructified by the spirit of faith
and the Church. There are even many people who do
not clearly distinguish keeping the parish files in
order from participation in holy Mass. They no longer
understand the essential difference between a Catholic association with a sacred aim and a religious
order which is a sacred entity. We often hear that all

this is meant for the glory of God, that it is all performed in a spirit of good intention, and that therefore it is all divine service. Of course, everything can be "consecrated," but this implies much more than a good intention. It implies making room in oneself for the reception of grace and exposing one's soul to the rays of Christ's visage; the accomplishment of all things not only for God but from the lived "I-thou" communion with Jesus, from the living membership in the Mystical Body of Christ, a membership which attains its summit in a life that has its sources in the holy Sacrifice of the Mass. And yet all this does not in any way efface the *objective* gradations in the relation that binds content and activity to the reign of God; it does not alter the essence of the service, its degree of proximity to the mystery which it possesses in itself because of its own content.

The clear sense of this great scale in the "service rendered to God," ascending until it reaches the unique service in spirit and truth, the offering of the sacrifice with Christ, through Christ and in Christ —this sense is the indispensable precondition for the consecration of all activities even if they are only indirectly linked to the reign of God. The man who lacks this sense, in spite of all his good intentions, will run the risk of beholding the sacred in the light of the profane, the supernatural in the light of the merely natural. He will even attend the holy Sacrifice of the Mass in an attitude of merely correct loyalty, substituting for the attitude of true, reverent obedience to God and the Church; he will not be able to distinguish this act from a superficial and indirect service rendered to the kingdom of God.

This element of *discretio* in the discernment of gradations in relations is also a mark of personality in its true sense; without it there can be no organic contact with the world of values, no formation of man through values, no true transformation into Christ.

This spirit of *discretio* is found everywhere in the Liturgy. Its structure and atmosphere clearly testify to this spirit, and the man who lives in the Liturgy grows organically into that spirit.

Let us recall the structure of the holy Mass. Behold the organic unfolding as it prepares for participation in the mystery. It is not a hurried march toward the great solemn central moment of Consecration. One is aware that certain stages must first be passed through. First the Introibo, mounting with the Confiteor to the altar of the Lord, the confrontation with God, the prayer for the forgiveness of sins, and then the centering of the Mass on the mystery of the feast of the day, as expressed in the Introit. Then the Kyrie, the great solemn cry for mercy; the adoring praise and thanksgiving offered to God in the Gloria; the Oration with the special allusion to the mystery of the feast of the day; the illumination and preparation of our spirit through the Epistle or the Lesson. Then comes the praise of the Gradual and the Alleluia, which rise as an echo to the Epistle; and then the even more solemn and deep illumination of the words of eternal life of the Gospel. The Credo resounds as a solemn response to the revelation contained in the words of the Lord through an expressly professed faith. All this is an organic preparation, an ascension toward the mystery. Then follows the Offertory in which we give ourselves up to Christ in order to be carried by Him and with Him to the Father; the raising of the bread and the wine; and the Lavabo which is another purification of a higher scale, performed alone this time by the priest directly on the threshold of the mystery. But we still stand in the world of symbols; it is still the priest as *representative* of Christ who acts, while we participate in his act.

As we approach the mystery more closely, we hear the Sursum corda. What a deep sense of the entirely new which is now on the point of beginning, what an inner elevation of our attitude to a new scale is now demanded! But before Christ enters into our midst to perform the sacrifice of the cross, the solemn praise and thanksgiving for the *magnalia Dei* must resound once more in the Preface culminating in the song of praise of the angels: Sanctus, Sanctus, Sanctus! Now the last veil drops, the authentic *actio* begins, the celebration of the mystery itself. First, the ultimate, highest unfolding of the consciousness of unity—the prayer for the holy Church, the pope, our bishop, all Christians, the loving glance directed to our dear ones and all those whom we want especially to carry in our prayers, the drawing of all into the mystery, the glorious vision of the Communion of Saints. And then, the world of symbols and of human acts fades away: Christ Himself, our Head, sacrifices Himself to His heavenly Father.

And, every time, from this highest sacrifice of the love of Christ to His heavenly Father, the blood of atonement streams into this world of suffering and sin; in the plenitude of light from the ineffable glory of this act, all darkness and twilight are once more illumined, and the entire world is drawn into this transfiguration.

Truly we behold in the holy Mass the primary image of the entire dramatic rhythm of being: stages must be traversed, there must be a "going-up," and an inner preparation for the utterance of an objectively genuine "Word." In the Consecration, in the real coming of Christ, we also behold the primal pattern of a full "now." Here we learn to know the moment charged with inner significance; here where time and eternity meet, we understand the ultimate essence of the full "now." But the further development of the holy Mass is just as organic as this ascension to the holy mystery. After we have participated expressly in the sacrifice of Christ, which reaches its climax in the prayer "Through Him, with Him and in Him (*Per ipsum, cum ipso et in ipso*)," the third part of the holy Mass, the sacrificial meal follows, solemnly initiated by the Pater noster, the Lord's Prayer. In the first part of the Pater, we once more are in the movement directed purely to the glorification of God, which until now has dominated the entire sacrificial act. In the second part of the Pater, we ask for the bread of life and the forgiveness of our sins, remembering and acknowledging that reciprocal love between men is the fundamental condition of union with God. Then the

Liturgy and Personality

Agnus Dei follows. We appeal to the mercy of Christ and ask for that peace which the world cannot give, which is however the indispensable condition for the sacrificial meal with Christ. Through the kiss of peace, we achieve the deepest preparation of our soul for the reception of the Body of the Lord, the dissolving of all that separates us and the unfolding of the love which binds us in Christ. Then comes the last confrontation with Christ, "Lord, I am not worthy (*Domine, non sum dignus*)." After this confrontation, the ineffably mysterious, loving turning to us of Christ is accomplished; it is the true reception of us into Him, the becoming One with Him, the fulfillment of the highest union of love with Him.

The specific theme of the holy Mass is now achieved. But the Mass does not suddenly break off here. The sublime prayers of thanksgiving follow, then the Communion, a chant of love in which the sacrament of the Eucharist is illumined by the special light of the mystery of the feast. Then comes the Postcommunion asking for the special grace of the feast as a consequence of the Eucharist for our life and our path toward eternity. It is only then that we hear the solemn dismissal: "Go, the Mass is ended (*Ite, missa est*)," and the "Thanks be to God (*Deo gratias*)." And still we linger as there follows the blessing of the priest, for us who are about to depart, and the blessing of the Logos Incarnated in the Gospel, in the reading of the first verses of the most mysterious of all the Gospels.

We find in the architecture of the holy Mass the primal image of the sense for the dramatic structure of a being, for its inner laws of development and the necessity of passing through the objectively-presented stages. But this sense of dramatic rhythm is also presented in many distinct elements of the Liturgy, as for instance in the incensing of the altar during the Kyrie and the Offertory, the incensing of the Gospel book, as well as in the blessing received by the deacon before the reading of the Gospel. We also find it in the purification of the chalice and the ablution of the hands after Communion, in the fact that the initial prayers are recited at the foot of the altar, as well as in many other details. These are not mere fortuitous creations of the rubrics, but the expression of the sense of different objective stages and what must take place in each of these before we dare pass on to the next one. They are the very embodiment of *discretio*.

We also find this spirit of *discretio* in the whole structure of the Breviary as well as in the articulation of the various Hours. They are all dominated by the clearly expressed sense of the rise, culminating point and aftermath, the organic unfolding of a single theme.

This spirit is reflected above all in the ritual of baptism and of holy orders. Observe the distinct gradation of the various phases of baptism which in the early ages of Christianity were also separate in time. The very fact that the reception of baptism is preceded by certain exorcisms is a deep and significant manifestation of this *discretio*, and we see this first of all in the divisions of the exorcisms and symbols into three stages. The first is the stage of the catechumens, the second that of the elect or *competentes*, and the third that of the neophytes, properly speaking. They are the three stages of inner ripening on the path leading to the reception of the sacrament itself. In each stage we find a corresponding exorcism. The separate symbols, acts and prayers within the three stages reflect in a unique fashion the ever-deepening preparation for the reception of the sacrament. In the first stage there comes after the dialogue, with its deep, fundamental questions and answers, the threefold breathing (*insufflatio*), the sign of the cross traced on the brow and heart, the laying on of hands, the salt placed on the catechumen's tongue. In the second stage there is the recitation of the Symbol of faith and the Pater noster, each recited together with the priest who lays the stole on the one to be baptized, thus introducing him into the Church. In the third stage there are the touching of the ears with saliva, while the priest utters the words: "*Ephpheta*! (Open!)," then the casting out of the devil, and the anointing with holy oil. Then only follows the actual baptism.

The Liturgy deeply expresses the sense of these various stages which are to be objectively passed through before the accomplishment of the sacrament. This is also reflected in the fact that though today even for the baptism of adults the entire baptismal rite is compressed in a short space of time, the gradations of the liturgical steps have been preserved intact. The candidate must pass through, though in a reduced space of time, the various stages of the path leading to the sacrament of baptism.

The same is true of holy orders. There are seven different orders, still separated in time even today, organically leading to the essential sacrament. What a *discretio* in the gradation of powers acquired by the various orders! How distinctly is there expressed here also that element of *discretio* in which the degrees of relationship with the kingdom of God are clearly distinguished in the various acts directed toward God. The divine service of the reading of the Epistle can be performed by one who is still only a subdeacon; the divine service of the reading of the Gospel and the preaching of a sermon is open only to the deacon. Whereas the latter is allowed to distribute holy Communion, the priest alone is allowed—indeed, he alone has the power—to offer the holy Sacrifice of the Mass.

This element of *discretio* was also expressed in the now extinct regulation concerning catechumens who were allowed to attend only the forepart of the Mass—before the beginning of the Offertory. Here we clearly distinguish the gradations in the closeness to God, the degrees of sacredness in the different kinds of divine service. As long as it was only the Word of God which was communicated, as long as the approach to God was established only through the natural spiritual faculties, the catechumens could remain in church. But only after baptism were they admitted to participation in the mystery proper, in which Christ Himself is present; only then could they take part in the *substantial, ontological contact* with God through the Eucharist. For only through baptism is this ontological link with Christ provided, that link which permits us to actually participate as members in the sacrifice of the Head.

Liturgy and Personality

This *discretio* is also clearly reflected in the distinction within the Liturgy between the sacraments and sacramentals. The wholly new degree of sacredness possessed by the sacraments as compared to the sacramentals is clearly expressed throughout the Liturgy. Both are forms of divine service, both are destined to glorify God, yet they are distinctly separate insofar as their objective link with God is concerned. And how deeply is the entire Liturgy penetrated with the sense of the depth of the level at which something must be performed. Its atmosphere of ultimate depth and of the presence of God, its profoundly sacred spirit, entirely irradiated by the Face of Christ, obviates the danger of our slipping onto the peripheral level so often presented by nonliturgical forms of devotion.

Everything in the Liturgy, even the singing, is formed by the spirit of Christ. What a world of ultimate greatness and truth, towering high above all petty predilections and entanglements, discloses itself in the solemnly uttered "O God, come to my assistance (*Deus in adjutorium meum intende*)"! It draws us into into the sacred realm where there is no place for anything profane.

And let us recall, on the other hand, the swamp of triviality and sentimentality into which certain modern religious hymns sink even though full of good and pious intentions. These hymns actually invite the faithful to drop into the superficial; they lead the outsider astray, for instead of offering him the true Face of Christ, as revealed in the Liturgy, they falsify it through a sugary sentimentality. Instead of drawing us out of our narrowness into the pure mysterious atmosphere of the King of Eternal Glory, instead of revealing to us the entire sweetness of His beauty, the mysterious splendor of the "fairest of the children of men," they lead us into a world of sentimentality and Philistine narrowness repulsive even from the natural point of view. Many hymns induce the faithful to abandon the level to which they have genuinely and validly moved by a deep religious experience, and to find refuge in the sphere of mere childhood memories; or else they incite to a profession of feelings of mere allegiance such as are typical of any Fourth of July gathering. This is not primarily an aesthetic question; it is, above all, a question of whether or not a hymn reflects the spirit of Christ, whether or not it is penetrated with a truly sacred atmosphere; it is a question of the level to which it leads us inwardly when we follow its spirit. Indeed it would be too naive to believe that the spirit of Christ is always truly reflected in everything which has been composed with the intention of edifying and is not heretical or immoral.

Let us also recall how many people celebrate Christmas in an atmosphere of pleasant childhood memories, with the burning lights of the Christmas tree, the mutual gifts, and so on. Such an atmosphere may be both delightful and charming when it is free of sentimentality. But it is removed by a deep gulf from the sphere of supernatural solemnity and majesty, from the realm of the mystery of the Incarnation as marked by the Invitatorium psalm of Christmas Matins. In the one case we find amiable harmlessness, in the other we behold adoring reverence before an inscrutable mystery. In the former case we run the risk of considering the birth of the God-man in a childish or harmless spirit, of transposing a sublime mystery of faith in to the sphere of purely human poetry. In the latter, as in the Introit of the Mass at dawn on Christmas Day, we enter the world of light: "A light shall shine upon us this day: for the Lord is born to us: and He shall be called Wonderful, God, the Prince of Peace, the Father of the world to come: of Whose reign there shall be no end (*Lux fulgebit hodie super nos: quia natus est nobis Dominus: et vocabitur Admirabilis, Deus, Princeps pacis, Pater futuri saeculi: cujus regni non erit finis*)."

And what a gulf between the Litany of the most Sacred Heart of Jesus, formed by the spirit of the Liturgy, and the modern hymns to the Sacred Heart! In the invocations of the Litany, as well as in the Office of the Feast of the Sacred Heart, the "mystery of the Incarnation" and the "mystery of Love" are revealed: "Heart of Jesus, in which dwelleth all the fullness of divinity! Heart of Jesus, in which are all the riches of wisdom and knowledge! Heart of Jesus, of Whose fullness we have all received! (*Cor Jesu, in quo habitat omnis plenitudo divinitatis! Cor Jesu, in quo sunt omnes thesauri sapientiae et scientiae! Cor Jesu, de cuius plenitudine omnes nos accepimus*!)." What a sublime, mysterious world of divine love envelops these words! How they feed on the mysteries of Revelation!

But in the modern hymns, the Heart of Jesus is stripped of the mystery of His divine and human nature in *one* person, and is considered in a purely natural light; it is not even contemplated in analogy to a naturally great and noble heart, but to a sentimental, sugary little human heart. Truly, in the Litany, something of the world of the God-man is *disclosed* to us; but in the modern hymns, this world is *closed* to our eyes; it is replaced by a world which is *unworthy* even from the natural point of view.

In the piety which is not formed by the Liturgy, the weight is easily shifted to that which is far less directly linked to God; it is shifted from the center to the periphery. For many, attendance at May devotions or rosary devotions appears as important as attendance at the holy Mass on weekdays. And even when they do not place them theoretically on the same scale, they actually give their preference to the devotions. Yes, many prefer to recite during Mass a prayer to St. Joseph or St. Anthony. For many, in the month of May, devotion to Mary overshadows Eastertime. For them this devotion to Mary stamps the day far more than does the Easter Cycle. For many, Solemn Benediction appears as central as the Mass. For many, the visit to a famous place of pilgrimage is a more solemn contact with the supernatural than that obtained by participating in the holy Sacrifice. They tremble in awe far more in touching a relic than in the preparation during which we tread before the Lord's altar. The man who is formed by the Liturgy possesses, on the contrary, the *discretio* which makes him recognize the degrees of closeness to mystery, distinguishing them even within the frame of the divine cult. He will fully affirm the venerable non-liturgical forms of piety; he will be fully aware of the charm which belongs to them in that they are secondary branches of the primordial; but he will see and experience them in their right place where objectively they stand.

The Liturgy teaches us to put everything in its right place in the realm of God; it bestows on us that *discretio* in its three dimensions, even regarding the natural order, through which our life becomes real and genuine, and we become true personalities. *A theoretical handling of the Liturgy*, or the turning of the Liturgy into a topic of research will not lead us to this formation. It can be had only by the true life in the Liturgy, its actual accomplishment, the inner formation of the spirit as expressed in the monastic Lauds of Monday:

> Christ Himself for food be given
> Faith become the cup of heaven
> Out of which the joy is quaff'd
> Of the Spirit's sobering draught.*

* *Christusque nobis sit cibus*
   Potusque noster sit fides
   Laeti bibamus sobriam ebrietatem Spiritus.

IX

The Spirit of Continuity in the Liturgy

One of the deepest and essential marks of man as a spiritual person is his continuity. This means not only the faculty of remembering the past, of looking back on what we have formerly known and experienced, but also the fact of knowing oneself to be *one* through the stream of time and of moments filled with the most varied contents. It means that man possesses not only one stratum of experience, the actual "here and now" which embraces only a limited content, but that he can retain on a deeper superactual stratum the knowledge of facts and values, and the response to them. Continuity is a presupposition for being fully a person, for the development of a person, for the rich world that a person may embody, as well as for all responsibility. If a man lived only separate moments without any link between them, if he did not know himself as the same being in the past and present, if all that he experienced and accomplished, as well as all that was revealed to him, sank back into nothingness before the actual contact with a new "now," he would be only a bundle of disconnected experiences. He would be deprived of the dimension of depth, and he would lack the essential element of being a person, an awakened being.

The power of continuity, like freedom, is the mark of every man as a spiritual person, but the degree of its unfolding may be extremely different.

There are unconscious men, always completely absorbed in the present moment. What has happened to them in the past, what moved and filled them, fades away as soon as a new, strong impression takes possession of them. They are capable of feeling these strong impressions, but these are not rooted in them, they do not become their unalterable possession and a background against which new impressions may stand out. In extreme cases, their impressions are juxtaposed without order and selection. The present always dominates the past, even when the content of the present is far more insignificant and mediocre. These people glide through life without developing from their contact with values and their experience of joys and sorrows. When their attention is drawn to their defects, they admit them for the moment but in the next moment everything is engulfed again. Such men are not really awake in spite of the force and vivacity of their impressions. They do not understand in particular that it is not enough to recognize at a given moment a principal truth, only to let it be engulfed by a succeeding one. They do not understand that it is necessary to retain this truth once and for all and to confront with it all new experiences. They fail to understand that each value disclosed to them demands not only a momentary affirmation, but that in addition it demands a superactual affirmation so that it may become a measure for all that life further offers. In such people, it is the advantage of intensity and power, which the present, actual experience possesses over the past, that turns the scale, and not the height of the value and the inner meaning and content of the experience. These men are dominated mostly by "fashion"; what is "in the air" at the present moment in their narrower and larger surroundings conquers them easily.

Besides this type of extreme discontinuity, we find another type of man who is accessible to deep experiences, for whom the truths and values disclosed to him have become a durable possession, but who does not resist the onrush of intense new impressions; the inner content accumulated in the past does not serve as a measure for these new impressions. These are the people who do not let what they possess in the depth of their soul become the principle of formation of the present situation. They may love another human being with a great and deep love, and be faithful to that person. But when powerful new impressions invade them, they let themselves be dominated and filled by them; the love which dwells within their depths is "forgotten" as long as the new impression lasts, and this indwelling love does not dominate and form the new situation from within. However, if the circumstances appeal once again to their love, when the beloved is once again with them, and nothing draws them into the periphery, the love which lives in their depths comes out again.

Here again, the power of the present and the freshness and power of new, unusual experiences exercise too great an influence. These persons, also, fail to give to acknowledged values and truths the full response due to them, to do justice in their lives to the essence of truth and the ageless unfading splendor of values. The man with a spirit of continuity, on the contrary, maintains super-actually all truths and values. He observes fully the response-to-value attitude; he possesses a complete understanding of the realm of values and their demands, he fully penetrates them; thus the values he has grasped and maintained become the natural background against which all new impressions stand out; not only do they arise against this background, but also their compatibility with it must be proved. The enchantment and glamour of novelty have as little hold on the man with a sense of continuity as mere habit has. The familiar and customary ceases to influence him as soon as it is discovered as valueless. The new, the freshly experienced, will not exercise any attraction on him if it is acknowledged to be without value. And even if these goods are not valueless, but belong to a sphere of goods which has been "surpassed" objectively by the higher goods he already possesses, he will not be chained down by them in spite of all their actuality. Just as the lesser value will recede in him of itself before a greater value, even so the new lesser value will have no advantage over the greater value already possessed.

The man without a sense of continuity fails also to understand contrition for wrongs committed in the past and the necessity of expressly revoking a wrong attitude of the past, of asking the forgiveness of those he has wounded, of expressly correcting past errors. He believes that all this belongs *to the past,* that if he behaves righteously in the present and commits no more errors, the essential has been achieved. The question of how much a thing belongs to the past or to the present plays an excessive role in his life.

The man with the spirit of continuity, on the contrary, understands that the disharmony caused by a wrong or a mistake in regard to fundamental truths does not cease to exist even when the wrong attitude and the error belong to the past.

It is obvious that continuity is an essential trait of true personality. For without full continuity there can be no inner unity of the person, no real growth, abundance, genuine contact with the objective logos, complete union with the realm of values, or the possibility of being innerly stamped with its seal. Without continuity, there is no real communion with persons, no real knowledge, faithfulness, trustworthiness or true happiness. For every real happiness implies precisely retaining what is hidden in the depths along with the actuality of the present moment. In continuity, man already anticipates a part of eternity. Continuity reflects the situation of eternity, an eternal "now" in which all is contained, in which we shall never be parted from the lived, complete contact with the plenitude of values which is in God, and in which the response-to-value will never be interrupted. Continuity is moreover a special condition of the transformation into Christ. What is the use of perceiving the call of God if we do not retain it in such fashion that it becomes the forming element of our life? If we let ourselves be so dominated by the impressions of the fleeting moment that Christ does not determine our attitude in life and does not impress His mark on it, we shall never be transformed even though our soul is filled with God as long as we are in church.

The organic development of divine life within us, in which we are allowed to participate through baptism, which attains its full personal reality in sanctity, necessarily presupposes continuity. If Christ must become the "form" of our soul even as the soul is the "form" of our body, our eyes must be superactually fixed on God. In every moment of our life, Christ must be the cornerstone against which all that is contrary to God must be shattered. He must be the light in which everything is seen and known, the measure which determines whether or not a thing should have a place in our life. Without continuity there is no organic ripening of the person, no growth, no ascension; life remains a series of beginnings, a perpetual dawn. The man with no sense of continuity denies God the response to His eternal unchangeableness, to the fact that *every moment* belongs to God. He ignores the fact that a continuous value-response is due to God, that each situation in life must be confronted with God, and that all our attitudes toward creatures and the problems of life must flow organically from this response. Here too, as in awakenedness, it is true that the more a man possesses continuity, the more he exists as a person.

A man who lacks the spirit of continuity escapes our grasp, his "consistency" is, as it were, always changing. We touch his depths at one time, we exchange with him a mutual glance of love, we speak to him a "valid" word, and he speaks it to us; at another time, a stranger stands before us, everything is forgotten, we grasp at the void when we try to take hold of him. Continuity is the foundation of all faithfulness: faithfulness to God, faithfulness to oneself and faithfulness to the human beings whom we love. Without it, there is no true communion. In continuity, the person does justice to the inner unity and consistency of being, and participates in them himself.

The Liturgy, more than anything else, is penetrated with the spirit of continuity, and dispenses this spirit to those who live in it. The daily repetition of the holy Sacrifice of the Mass and the Hours is a specific expression of continuity, of the sense of the necessity for always sacrificing to God, Who contains all values, so as to praise and thank Him. The frequent repetitions

in the Liturgy, which certain people consider unnecessary and wearisome, testify precisely to this continuity. The Gloria Patri must accompany each psalm
because our prayer must again and again turn expressly to the mystery of mysteries, the Trinity; the
superactually existent adoration must be actualized
anew. Due account is here rendered to God, Who is
always equally new, equally significant, ever de-
manding worship, love, adoration. How often is repeated the ''O God, come to my assistance (*Deus in
adjutorium meum intende*).'' What a spirit of continuity in
the awareness that this supplication is, at every moment, timely! How often does the Confiteor return! The
Credo which is so frequently repeated manifests a sense
of the necessity for continuity in our faith. This continually renewed realizing of revelation educates us in
continuity. How often is the Alleluia repeated, and the
Hodie of Christmas! In the Liturgy, we are immersed in
the world of eternity where there is no room for the
power of the habitual or the sensationally new. The unfading splendor of God's eternal beauty and holiness,
the eternally new *sweetness* of the God-man are always
equally timely, always equally thematic.

Again, what an expression of continuity in the re-
current rhythm of the Liturgical Year! Every year
there is the same unfolding of longing in Advent, the
same rejoicing and thanksgiving at Christmas, the
same transfigured exultation at Easter! What a spirit
of continuity in the fact that a saint who lived two
thousand years ago is venerated today as much as a
recently canonized one! In this we see that the same

response is eternally due to the *magnalia Dei* in the saints, that we must maintain this response, that it must be not only a response uttered once, but an abiding one. The holiness of a martyr who lived eighteen hundred years ago is today as much a motive of joy, thanksgiving and praise as the holiness of St. Thérèse of the Child Jesus who lived in our own time. The gradation of the feasts of saints is determined by the importance of the saint, or by his role in the work of salvation, but never by the time which separates him from us. The always equal actuality of the martyrdom of St. Stephen, St. Paul's conversion, the liberation of St. Peter, which we celebrate each year with an undiminished joy, is a triumphant affirmation of the timeless significance of all that is a true value. In the Liturgy there truly breathes the spirit of God ''for Whom a thousand years are as one day.'' What a continuity in the firmly molded forms of all the prayers which we constantly repeat! It is not necessary for us to speak new words to God, but only to maintain the objectively adequate, ''valid'' word in the prayer of the Church and to participate in it always more deeply and originally.

Thus the Liturgy itself is a great actualization of continuity, a participation in the adoring love of the Son for His heavenly Father which always remains the same. The man who lives in the Liturgy acquires the spirit of continuity; his relations also will become continuous with all true values which speak to us of God's glory; so also his relations with other men, the community, knowledge, the world of beauty, nature and art.

Liturgy and Personality

Through continuity is achieved the *true simplicity of the person*, which in spite of all differentiations manifests ultimate unity because it maintains the deepest and crowning value-response, the response to God, which forms all the other value-responses. In spite of its richness and inexhaustible differentiation, the Liturgy is filled with this simplicity. The man formed by the Liturgy is simple because he lives from God and performs everything in God, because he performs everything through Christ, with Christ and in Christ. He is no longer under the spell of the present moment, of whatever is new; the charm of novelty has lost its power to distract and scatter him. Over his life is written ''Christ yesterday, today and forever (*Christus heri, hodie et in saecula*).''

X

The Organic Element in the Liturgy

It is with satisfaction that we frequently encounter in our days a longing for the organic and a revulsion against all that is artificial, superimposed from the outside or merely arbitrary. Unfortunately, this longing for the organic often leads to certain deviations, such as a deification of the vital and a distrust of the spiritual in man. The spirit is held responsible for all that is artificial. This longing has led to the cult of the subconscious and to a disdain for the conscious. All that takes place of itself, without the cooperation of freedom, is emphasized in man. These deviations are based on a false antithesis of the organic and the inorganic. The true essence of the organic is an all-pervading fullness of meaning. It has two opposites: the mechanical, deprived of meaning; and the artificial, which has a meaning-content, but is super-imposed from the outside. A mere sum of people is a mechanical structure, deprived of meaning. An association, such as a corporation, has a content of meaning, but this has been superimposed from the outside, and has given rise to an artificial structure. A family, on the contrary, is an organic structure because it is a community formed from within and originating from what is central in man. A machine possesses a content of meaning, but is an artificial structure. A work of art, on the contrary, is an *organic* structure. The sphere of the mechanical is dominated by the categories of quantity, and mere juxtaposition. The sphere of the organic is dominated by the interpenetration of the parts. In the artificial, in spite of the meaning imposed from the outside and a kind of interpenetration of the parts, the juxtaposition remains. The more organic a structure, the simpler it is in spite of its differentiation and content of meaning. The more inorganic it is, *the more its simplicity means poverty*.

The organism, from which the word "organic" originates, is a typical example of an organic unity built up from an inner center of meaning; but it is not by any means the ultimate pattern of the organic. The spiritual person as such is *a unity far more penetrated with meaning*, and far more differentiated; yet it embodies this principle of interpenetration to such an extent that it is truly simple. The spiritual person as a whole is far more contained in his attitudes and acts than the organism in its members and organs. By virtue of his being conscious, capable of knowledge and meaningful responses, the spiritual person is far more filled with meaning than a mere organism. His contact with being, his capacity to penetrate it, to participate in it spiritually and possess it through knowledge, his conscious touching of value even in the humblest response-to-value belong far more to organic structure than does the brutal causal contact between the living organism and the surrounding world. The spiritual person reaches the summit of the organic, the nonartificial, in the *free* "Yes" of the sanctioned response-to-value, in the explicit, comprehending penetration of value, in the ultimate concerting with its inner rhythm. In the sanctioned response-to-value, the real giving of self is first reached, for only here does the conscious center of the person, fully awake, conform itself to the value. The way in which the value touches our spirit, and engenders our answering "Yes," above all in sanctioned love, is organic in the highest degree, far removed from the mechanical and artificial in the whole natural order.

The world of the artificial presupposes, of course, a spiritual person. In nature, there is only the mechanical and the organic, that which is poor in meaning or filled with meaning from within. Only man as a spiritual person can create a unity the meaning of which has been superimposed from the outside, as in the case of all fabricated objects, and especially the machine. But though the spirit is the presupposition of the machine, and nothing artificial can be produced by life alone, yet the spirit itself is that which is the most unartificial of all. All the essential, central attitudes of the person are specifically organic; organic too in their meaningful springing into existence, especially in the case of love. But the will also, as such, is something organic, and responds to a fact possessing a value with a "Thou shalt exist!" A considerable part of what is created by the person is also specifically organic—all the assertions of real knowledge, all genuine works of art and all culture.

Only a relatively restricted realm is inorganic, such as the sphere of technique in the broadest sense of the word, civilization, certain community structures such as clubs, and so forth. Yet this artificial character does not represent a disvalue, but only an inferior value, at a lower level in respect to the organic, just as the mechanical in inorganic nature is not a disvalue. In its own realm the artificial character is legitimate.

The definite disvalue of the artificial begins only at that point where it is introduced into a sphere which is organic in its meaning and essence. Thus, for instance, when we attempt to "produce" extraneously in ourselves a joy which must originate spontaneously, which must be "generated" through the contact of our spirit with the value. If our will commands an action, this is the adequate way for the springing into existence of the action. But when our will "commands" love instead of seeking only to remove the obstacles which lie in its way, when we command love instead of opening ourselves to the value of the beloved and seeking to approach the person from within in order to allow love to arise in us organically, then our attitude is inorganic. This does not mean however that we must not *desire* to love God and our neighbor. Our soul, of course, must be constantly filled with this desire, but we must understand that the path by which this aim may be truly attained, is a roundabout way. This way is the normal one demanded by the meaning of love. We behave inorganically if, in a fit of impatience and overestimation of our will-power, we seek to stimulate love directly, as one stimulates a gesture or an action. The so-called "acts of love," which are "produced" by force, are inorganic acts far removed from genuine love which is "generated" in us. We must humbly admit that the greatest and most important function of our will consists in a very indirect preparation of the ground of love. Whenever we violate *discretio* and refuse to obey the inner laws of development, and attempt to "make" something from outside with the help of our will, our attitude is inorganic, artificial in the sense of an explicit disvalue.

A specifically typical example of the negative, inorganic attitude is found in that of some women who long for a child before they long for a husband. It is out of the love for the husband that the longing for a child organically arises, as the longing for the highest symbol of the unity of husband and wife. To desire this fruit of the unity of love without this unity itself, shows a lack of *discretio* and reveals the fact that one artificially places foremost an attitude which must organically follow, and not precede, the other one.

The absence of the longing for a child in marriage, the rejoicing even in the fact that one has remained childless in marriage is also an inorganic attitude, for it breaks off the deeply meaningful and mysterious link between love and the coming of a new human being into the world.

It is a specific mark of the true personality that everything in him takes place in an organic manner, in the contact of his spirit with values. His joy, his love, are begotten organically; his single acts, such as his acts of thanksgiving, praise and glorification, grow organically out of this inner plenitude; his attitude in each situation originates organically from his basic attitude; his ascension and ripening toward sanctity, organically growing out of this basic attitude, penetrate all the spheres of his person.

The way to true personality does not lead through the formation of a technique of the will, a decomposition of life into a series of separate, cramped acts, a partitioning of our relations with God into momentary, inorganically linked, quantitatively multiplied little sacrifices, renunciations, appealing glances, and intentions. It does not lead through a petty decomposition of God's commandments into innumerable rules dominating every situation in life from the outside. The way to true personality leads rather through the opening of oneself in the depths, the exposing of oneself to the sun of God; it means being filled with joy by the glory of God, longing to see and to know oneself in His light, in confrontation with Him. This path leads through a love enkindled by the divine beauty of Christ, a love which gives ardor and power to one's will to walk in the ways of the Lord. It implies making room in oneself for the life implanted in us by baptism, giving God the opportunity to speak in us, ''watching'' before the Lord. It means especially the clear understanding that we are impotent to form Christ in our soul *by our own efforts*, but that the Lord must transform us; that we cannot save our soul by our own power, but only by the power of Christ. It requires prayer for the right thoughts and decisions, prayer for love, grasping the fact that our task is only a free cooperation with grace, letting ourselves be transformed by God. The way to true personality is not through the application of a number of pedagogical rules to our own person, a number of acts which are not accomplished for their own sake but only as a means for a determined aim. What is necessary is the growing into God through value-responses valid in themselves, demanded as such, and not intended as means.

It is along this path that the Liturgy *leads* us. In opposition to certain forms of extraliturgical piety, in which transformation is sought through the formation of a technique of the will, the Liturgy unfolds before our spiritual eyes the glory of the Lord. In the experience of the Liturgical Year, the Liturgy reveals the true Face of Christ in its ineffable mysterious beauty; in all its symbols it envelops us with the air of the supernatural; in its chants it immerses us in the atmosphere of a continual Epiphany of the Lord; and in the union of our spirit with this world, the Liturgy awakens in us holy love and joy, holy longing, and the immovable will to serve God in everything.

In other forms of piety, a military and hence mechanical discipline imposed on life divides the day into innumerable acts of the will and into a succession of deliberate emotions. Through a series of separate acts from without, having, as it were, a kind of autosuggestive character, our life is transformed according to this discipline. The Liturgy, on the contrary, places uppermost the fundamental attitude to God and the enduring being of man; and it is from this fundamental attitude that the separate acts must grow organically. Certain forms of asceticism regard the blossoming of the supernatural as conditioned by a forced crushing of nature, by the application of a stoic indifference to all earthly goods. On the contrary, the Liturgy is organically linked to our nature, and leads us by organic degrees of transformation toward the supernatural. In the Liturgy, too, of course, we die with Christ in order to arise with Him; in the Liturgy, too, we die to the world in order to live to God; but this dying is an organic process, it does not mean a killing off and a forced denial of nature, an artificial benumbing, but an inner emptying of oneself for God. This way of linking nature with the supernatural is precisely typical of the distinction between the organic and the inorganic path of the transformation into Christ. An example of this is the attitude toward suffering in prayer. When St. Teresa asked God for suffering in order to be still more closely linked with the suffering of Christ, this was an organic consequence of the degree of her communion with God and the special graces in which she participated. Her prayer is therefore true, valid, and of a sublime greatness. But if we wanted to begin our transformation and our conforming to Christ by asking for suffering, this would be an inorganic, forced and untrue attitude. This would be to behave as if we had no nature. The organic way in praying to God is to ask Him to protect us from sufferings and ordeals if it please His holy will to do so; but if in His divine providence God chooses to send us sufferings, we should ask Him to give us the strength to bear them in the spirit of Christ. Such precisely are the prayers of the Liturgy.

In the Litany of All Saints on Holy Saturday, we pray: "From plague, famine, and war, deliver us, O Lord (*A peste, fame et bello, libera nos, Domine*)"; "From lightning and tempest, deliver us, O Lord (*A fulgure et tempestate, libera nos, Domine*)."

In many petitions we ask for the turning away of earthly evils. Thus, for instance, in the prayer of the Nineteenth Sunday after Pentecost: "Almighty and merciful God, in Thy goodness put far from us all that may work us harm: that alert alike in mind and body, we may readily devote ourselves to the doing of Thy holy will." Even in the Canon of the Mass, in the prayer after the Pater noster, we pray: "Deliver us, we beseech Thee, O Lord, from all evils, past, present, and to come (*Libera nos, quaesumus, Domine, ab omnibus malis, praeteritis, praesentibus, et futuris*)."

Certain votive Masses are also intended to avert earthly evils, as for instance the Masses for the sick and for pilgrims and travelers. In the "Occasional Prayers," likewise, we find such petitions for the averting of evil, while other prayers ask for the grace to accept in the right spirit whatever is sent by God.

In many forms of piety, which have not originated in the spirit of the Liturgy, the accent is placed on separate elements, and there is an arbitrary isolation of certain religious attitudes, as, for instance, an ascetic attitude toward the goods received from God, the Father of Lights—an attitude which often neglects the value-response of gratitude and acceptance which is due for these goods. The great danger of being lost in created goods, a danger implied in our fallen nature, is stressed so much that every situation in which a created good is granted us is considered an occasion for asceticism. Thus it is recommended that we close our eyes before a beautiful landscape and take advantage of this occasion to offer a sacrifice to God; this attitude is recommended instead of the due response to the glory of God revealed in this creation—a response of joy and enthusiasm, of seeking God in this beauty, and inwardly joining in the objective praise rising from this beauty toward God.

In other cases, it is recommended that we inquire on every occasion: "Of what use is this for my salvation?" This question must naturally be distinguished from the one asked by St. Aloysius: "How does this stand in relation to eternity? (*Quid hoc ad aeternitatem?*)," which is a seeing of all created things in the light of God, and should help us precisely to see the object in its true value. The first question implies far more the consideration of all objects as a mere means of obtaining eternal salvation, the limitation of our interests to their usefulness for the task of our salvation. It takes the place of that other attitude in which one first of all rejoices in the value one encounters and affirms the greatness and bounty of God revealed in it. The Liturgy knows nothing of this overemphasis and isolation of a certain religious attitude, which, as such, is justified and good. Everything in the Liturgy is put in the place where, by its value, it belongs; everything is seen in the great perspective of the total classical relationship between God and man, everything appears in its organic harmony. Next to the "Lord our God, how admirable is Thy name (*Domine Deus noster, quam admirabile est nomen tuum*)," we find the "Lord, Lord, who shall stand it (*Domine, Domine, quis sustinebit*)"; next to the Gloria, we find the Confiteor; next to the "King of dreadful majesty (*Rex tremendae majestatis*)," the "Fount of pity, save thou us (*Salva nos fons pietatis*)." But this leads to another essential and typical trait of the Liturgy, distinguishing it from all extra-liturgical forms of piety: its classical character.

XI

The Classical Spirit in the Liturgy

He who penetrates the Liturgy with open eyes and heart would like to exclaim, "O Truth, Truth, Truth!" Everything is pervaded here with the breath of the Holy Ghost, everything is irradiated with the *lumen Christi*, everything testifies to the eternal Logos. All semblance, wavering, illusion, all that is false, extravagant, or cramped is dispelled. The Liturgy is the primal image of all that is *classical*, in the highest sense of the word.

All the features of the Liturgy which we have so far discovered disclose to our spiritual eyes its deeply classical nature: the spirit of true communion and of reverence; the truth, everywhere affirmed, that an adequate response is due to every value, together with the sense for the hierarchy of values which this implies; the light of awakenedness which irradiates the Liturgy; its spirit of *discretio* and continuity, its deeply organic structure.

The *discretio* especially, and the organic structure, are deeply linked to this classical character. It is indeed the essence of the classical to see everything in the place where it objectively belongs, all the dimensions clearly revealed, nothing shifted or concealed, everything unfolded according to its logos and in its organic structure; there is no place in it for extravagance, romantic embellishment, or ambiguity. The classical spirit sees the world in its dimension of depth, its luminous plenitude of value, as a manifestation of God. It excludes all bluntness, all seeing from without, all subjective misinterpretation, all pragmatic distortion. In a word, to be classical means that everything is rooted in the objective logos and is in full conformity with it.

This conformity with the objective logos is also a mark of personality. In the beginning of this work, it was pointed out that in the purely natural order the man with personality is already distinguished from the average man precisely by the fact that the classical human attitudes are achieved by him in their unbroken and undistorted intensity, depth and plenitude. A true personality always gives to the essential precedence over the unessential; he makes an impression on us which derives not from any fortuitous peculiarities, but from the fact that all that corresponds to the true essence of man is fully developed in him;

he lives and has his being in the metaphysical situation of man.

The classical man is concerned with genuine problems. He acknowledges the danger of sin, realizes his need of salvation, knows the weakness and frailty of his nature, is filled with the longing for truth, communion and love, feels the insufficiency of that which is created, aspires to the absolute, and is "restless until he rests in God." The unclassical man is absorbed in illusory problems, problems which originate in a subjective cramp; he is tormented by self-engendered problems. The difference between the classical and the unclassical is reflected even in the sphere of sin, imperfection and error. Every sin, of course, every deviation from objective value, every error is unclassical in itself. But this difference between the classical and the unclassical is repeated analogously in the sphere of error and sin. If, in the error or in the sin, there is to be found, nevertheless, a certain pertinence to the objective logos; if real, central problems are at stake, then even disvalue and error can have a certain classical character. If the deviation occurs at a place in our fallen nature which is objectively corrupted, this secondary classical character can still be found. The more fortuitous, arbitrary, eccentric and ungenuine a sin or error is, the more unclassical it is.

Thus, for instance, materialism is a classical error, founded on something which presents an objective difficulty for fallen man, because it is the result of spiritual inertia, of the incapacity for "conspiring" with being. Pragmatism, on the contrary, the theory which reduces truth to utility, is so artificial, so far-fetched, that it must be defined as an unclassical error. Gluttony, impurity, laziness, pride, the craving for power, hardheartedness, ambition and cruelty are classical sins; they are the antithesis of central values; they are the true opposites of positive values; they are linked to the primal human weaknesses and disorders which have arisen from original sin. To sin out of boredom, sophistication, mere infatuation with the sensational, the feeling of self-importance caused by sin, or because of nerves and hysteria is specifically unclassical. The cult of idols in its literal sense is a classical sin; the atheism of the enlightened is an unclassical one. Sufferings from physical sickness, poverty, unrequited love, separation from the beloved, or the great separation of death are classical sufferings. Sufferings from boredom, self-hatred, one's inferiority complex, the impossibility of giving up self-analysis and falling in love are specifically unclassical sufferings. This does not mean that unclassical sins are worse than the classical ones. We should not make the mistake of considering the relative "classicism" of certain sins as a value and lending them the glamour of grandeur and originality. Such a conception would be specifically unclassical. It would be a sign of aestheticism, the typical unclassical attitude.

To begin with, every sin ultimately considered is piteous, ugly, foul, petty, lamentable. Secondly, the question as to whether or not something possesses glamour and grandeur is quite unessential when we are concerned with its degree of moral disvalue, with how much it offends God. Unclassical sins actually are usually the less grave ones.

It is important to understand that people who are burdened with unclassical sins are already warped and desubstantialized in their spiritual powers, and that they must first become spiritually healthy before they can become holy. Being cut off from the objective logos, they are also less capable of offending God than those who are healthy, but in a certain sense they are further removed from the saint since they must not only be converted and pass from hostility and bluntness to values, to a response to them, but they also must be formally changed and pass from a perverted structure to a normal one, from a formal absence of contact with the world of being to living contact with it, from ungenuineness to genuineness.

Our present age is especially rich in unclassical men, unclassical problems and unclassical conceptions of the cosmos. The tendency to make our nerves responsible for all morally negative wrongs such as irritation, egocentricity, bluntness, instead of imputing them to our own freedom is specifically unclassical. What an extraordinary difference in the contemplation of our defects and the problem of sin in general, between the *Confessions* of St. Augustine and certain modern autobiographies or the works of modern psychiatrists and eugenicists, who reduce everything to a question of environment and heredity! What a great classical conception of the cosmos is that of St.

Liturgy and Personality

Augustine! But what an unclassical leveling of the world is revealed in the modern conception, what a denial of the essential and the original, of the true features of the world!

It is also unclassical to accent the interest in why a person has spoken, in his psychological motives, instead of in what has been said and whether it is true or false. No less unclassical is the widespread attitude in philosophy according to which only immanent criticism is applied to great thinkers instead of the verification of their thoughts from the point of view of objective truth.

What an unclassical modern conception, to take another example, is contained in the self-styled "functionalism" which reduces the cosmos, irradiated by values, to a mere tissue of aims, to a sum of neutral, immanent laws, excluding the truly thematic content as an unnecessary, subjective superstructure, a theory which sees the cosmos systematically from without.

It is not, however, only the distorted, unauthentic man who is unclassical, but also the "hard-boiled" individual, that is, the man who disdains the spheres of knowledge, art, or the love between a man and a woman as more or less romantic fantasies and luxuries; the man who considers economic and political problems, or problems of civilization, as the only really *serious* things in life. He too lacks the necessary "organs" for the perception of the central sphere of life. He is just as unclassical as the aesthete. A specific case of unclassicism is that of the conventional man, of the bourgeois, whose attitude is exclusively influenced by public opinion; the one who belittles the cosmos and renders everything harmless and desubstantialized; the man who is capable only of tame, conditional attitudes toward all things; the entirely unheroic man who does not want to spoil his relations with anyone and lives by the social image which he enjoys by reason of his reputation.

The classical man is opposed to all these types. He is the spiritually healthy man, the man who stands in full primal relation to spheres of life, who knows the world in its true dimensions, whose response to values possesses inner plenitude, and is heroically unconditional. He understands that there is something great in the knowledge of truth; he grasps the seriousness implied in a great work of art; he clearly sees the depth of greatness of the true love between a man and a woman, the mystery of the birth of a new human being through the love-union of man and woman, the glorification of God in every love-communion in Jesus, as in a saintly friendship. He sees the great symbols and analogies which penetrate the entire cosmos; he sees, first of all, everything in the light of Christ, in the light of the ultimate truth, in its breadth and depth, in its objective hierarchy; and his responses are in harmony with this. He is, in other words, and as we have said already, the man who is inwardly conformed to the objective logos.

In the fulfillment of the Liturgy, which (more than anything else) breathes the classical spirit, man is placed in the truth: he achieves the true, valid relation to God and the world; and by this he becomes free from all bogging-down in the dead-ends of useless thoughts and illusory problems; free from one-sidedness, extravagance, self-deception, repression, and artificial evasions; he does not live in a world of subjective illusions. What a contrast to all extravagances, to all false spiritualism is presented by the Liturgy! The prayers speak clearly and definitely of the frailty of man, the wretchedness of our souls, and our misery. Nothing is idealistically embellished, nothing disavowed, neither our dependence nor our weakness and unreliableness. How classical is the Liturgy's attitude also toward the sphere of sex. It speaks quite openly of the birth of man in the Ave Maria, in the versicles after the prayer Sacrosanctae: "Blessed the womb which carried the Son of the eternal Father; And blessed the breasts which gave suck to Christ the Lord *(Beata viscera, quae portaverunt aeterni Patris Filium; Et beata ubera, quae lactaverunt Christum Dominum)*."

What an inner freedom in the question of the Blessed Virgin, "How shall this be done because I know not man?" which figures in the Gospels of so many feasts dedicated to the Mother of God! What a grand audacity in the application of the Canticle of Canticles in the Liturgy! What a contrast to all prudishness, to the pretense that the sphere of sex does not exist, and to that hushing-up still encountered in Catholic circles! What a spirit of truthfulness, a clear sight of all things *in conspectu Dei*! It is sufficient to recall the hymn of Compline and many other passages of the Liturgy.

On the other hand, we never find in the Liturgy the disastrous, purely neutral treatment of the sphere of sex which is often met with today and is considered by many as a sign of progress—that irreverent attitude which speaks of that sphere without any understanding of its character of mystery, of the mysterious beauty which it possesses as a sphere of fulfillment of the highest union of love, or of its deepest symbolical expression. There is the same lack of understanding of the mystery of the coming into existence of a new human being, and of the *mysterium iniquitatis*, the mystery of sin, implied in its abuse. Such an attitude is also typically unclassical. It is the result of the leveling, neutralizing, profoundly artificial attitude of the self-styled "functionalism," which in reality is the most unobjective of all attitudes. There is nothing of that kind to be found in the Liturgy. This sphere is considered here in its two genuine aspects: as the danger-zone of sin, and a mysterious, sanctioned fulfillment of mutual love, of love as expressed in the passages of the Canticle of Canticles in the Liturgy, and in the rite of marriage.

In the Liturgy, we are not only enveloped in the classical, the genuine, in contrast with all extravagance and self-delusion, but we are also enveloped in the classical as the opposite of all one-sidedness. It is the classical character of the all-embracing totality of truth. The Liturgy breathes an air that is free from all local peculiarities, from all that is fortuitous and dependent on time. Above all, it does not overemphasize *one* religious truth. It takes into account the multiple aspects of supernatural truth. In it there is no antithesis between the historical and pneumatic Christ; the mysterious unity of Christ the man and the eternal logos clearly appears; it lets our eyes behold God's epiphany in the Son of the Blessed Virgin, the Incarnation of the blessed Word, at a definite historical moment, in a definite place, from the tribe of David.

In the numerous texts of the Gospel, which penetrate the entire Liturgy, in the feasts of the Liturgical Year, Christ's humanity unfolds before our eyes in its full concreteness and reality. In the Epistles and readings of the holy Sacrifice of the Mass, in the Lessons of Matins, in the Psalms, in the action of the Sacrifice, in the beginning of St. John's Gospel, in the rites of the sacrament, the Messias appears in His divine mystery: the Mediator, the Savior, the Logos made flesh. These two elements do not rise before us unlinked, juxtaposed, but in that ultimate reciprocal interpenetration corresponding to the two in one Person. Christ does not stand before us at one time as a man and another time as God, but as the God-man, as a man whose every word, every attitude, every act, and whose entire visible human being testifies to His divinity, and is an epiphany of God.

Today, one often opposes to a Christocentric piety, in which Christ is adored as the God-man, the theocentric piety in which through Christ and with Christ we adore the Father. In Christocentric piety, Christ so to speak stands before us and looks at us, while we at the same time look into His Face. In theocentric piety,

Christ also stands before us, but He is turned toward the Father, on the summit of humanity, so to speak, leading us to the Father and preceeding us on that way. In Christocentric piety, we adore Christ. In the-ocentric piety, Christ is the mediator, the Head of humanity, our brother. Though the piety of certain ages, as for instance that of modern times, is often one-sided, Christocentrically-directed, today the theocentric attitude is observed in opposition to the Christocentric one, and considered the only correct and genuinely Catholic one.

In reality, it is a mistake to oppose these two forms of relationship with Christ. Christ is both the eternal Word of the Father addressed to us, God's epiphany, and the mediator between us and God, our Head through whom alone we may adequately adore God. Christ eternally turns His face both toward the Father *and* toward us. He is not only one who leads us to God like Moses; He not only stands at the side of humanity looking up at God together with humanity and leading us to God, but He also stands before us, as the self-revelation of God, as He who speaks to Philip: "Philip, he that seeth me, seeth the Father also," and of whom St. John says: "And we saw His glory, glory as of the only-begotten of the Father, full of grace and truth (*Et vidimus gloriam ejus, gloria quasi unigeniti a Patre, plenum gratiae et veritatis*)."

Our bond of union with Christ is not only a "we-Thou communion," in which the exclusive Thou is God the Father; our bond of union is also an "I-thou communion." In the giving of ourselves by love to

Christ, in becoming one with Him, we are drawn into the most Holy Trinity.

Though our "we-communion" with Christ, our membership in His Mystical Body is ontologically constituted in supernatural fashion through baptism, it would, nevertheless, remain dead without the giving of ourselves through faith and love to Christ. Thus especially the full transformation into Christ will never be achieved in us without the "I-thou" communion with Christ.

Once again we find in the Liturgy both these aspects in their mysterious interpenetration. In the holy Mass, we sacrifice with Christ, our Head; He is turned toward the Father, and He does not turn away from the Father when in holy Communion His Face is turned toward us; and through this communion of love with Him we are received through His holy humanity into His Godhood. At Christmas, and especially on the feast of the Epiphany, Christ stands before us as the God become man, as the Word of the Father, which He addresses to us. The Christmas Preface expresses this with a particular clarity: "For by the mystery of the Word made flesh, the light of Thy glory hath shone anew upon the eyes of our mind so that while we acknowledge Him as God seen by man we may be drawn by Him to the love of things unseen (*Quia per incarnati Verbi mysterium, nova mentis nostrae oculis lux tuae claritatis infulsit: ut dum visibiliter Deum cognoscimus, per hunc in invisibilium amorem rapiamur*)." In the Collects, Christ stands once more as mediator before us. In the Psalms also we join in His prayer to the Father. In certain hymns, as in the "Jesu dulcis memoria," the adoration of Christ prevails.

Here these two aspects are not juxtaposed but organically interpenetrated, and especially in the holy Mass and Communion; they are indeed but two aspects of one and the same mystery, the Incarnation.

Concerning the saints, these two aspects are analogously found in the Liturgy. Sometimes we are united with the saints in the great communion of the Mystical Body of Christ and adoring with them: we face God; at other times we lift our eyes from the valley of tears to the heavenly Jerusalem, and we behold the saints reflecting Christ and manifesting God. We see the saints as our intercessors, and also as witnesses to the *magnalia Dei*, as a reflection of God's glory, as persons in whom Christ lives, who radiate Him and manifest God through Him.

Both aspects are of a classical nature. Both find their full expression in the Liturgy. In the prayers of the Canon, *Communicantes* and the *Nobis quoque peccatoribus*, both aspects appear in their interpenetration. In the Suscipe Sancte Pater of the Offertory, the gaze lifted to the heavenly Jerusalem prevails. The fact that there are feasts dedicated to the saints, in which the holy Mass is said in their honor, reflects once more the aspect of the heavenly Jerusalem. This is the aspect reflected in the Introit of the feast of All Saints: "Let us all rejoice in the Lord, celebrating a festival day in honor of all the saints (*Gaudeamus omnes in Domino, diem festum celebrantes sub honore Sanctorum omnium*)." In the Collects of the Mass, on the contrary, in which we ask God to harken to our prayers because of the saints' merits, we are again directed to the other aspect.

The classical element of the Liturgy is especially expressed in the totality of truth. The man formed by the Liturgy will not fall into the exaggeration and isolation of one truth only; he will not cling to one aspect only; he will live from an organic, synoptic vision and the entire plenitude of supernatural truth.

The Liturgy does not display one particular form of piety among many others. It is the piety of the Church itself, the praying Christ. Actually there is no specific liturgical piety; for Liturgy is the accomplishment of the Mystical Body of Christ itself, of true relationship with God. True mysticism and asceticism belong organically to the Liturgy as parts of the general relationship of man with God. They not only present no contradiction, but they flow moreover directly out of the liturgical act. Validly performed, the Liturgy naturally includes asceticism; it is sufficient to recall Lent, the Ember Days, the Vigils, the immanent mortification involved in the proper physical comportment during prayer. And, still more, the Liturgy performed with full consciousness includes meditation and contemplation. Let us recall Matins and its Lessons. Indeed, those who really understand the spirit of the Liturgy will also understand the necessity of an explicit *inner prayer*, of the complete emptying of oneself before God, standing before Him, harkening, making room for God in us, and giving God a chance to speak in us. They will know how difficult for our fallen nature is recollection, emerging from the tensions centered on the coming moment, from the frenzy of getting everything over with so that we can rush toward that which comes next. They will become aware of the danger of drawing the liturgical act into the turmoil of activism, and accomplishing it as a mere duty. But the highest goal for the practice of inner prayer, namely, dwelling in the presence of God, will reach its climax precisely in the entirely awake and ultimate participation in the Liturgy. Here also is to be found the primal source of all true mysticism, that is to say of the conscious, grace-inspired experience of the most Holy Trinity in us.

The organic matrix for all asceticism is the confrontation with God achieved in the Liturgy; and so too the mystery performed in the Liturgy is the organic primal basis of all mysticism. From the Liturgy everything receives its inner classical form. The asceticism and contemplation achieved fully in the Liturgy are the highest of all. It is not the ascetic aspect as such, nor the longing to touch and experience the Holy Trinity dwelling in us through baptism which prevail here as something isolated. It is mortification, as a direct corollary to the life of Christ, which is achieved in the Liturgy, and mysticism, as the true *experience* of the mystery (if it is granted, of course, as a free gift of God), which comes from participation in the glorification of God through Christ, with Christ and in Christ.

Should we not fall on our knees before God in adoring thanksgiving for the ineffable gift of the Liturgy when we consider the narrowness and limitation of man, and how easily even faithful Catholics of good will slip away from the spirit of Christ; when we consider further how even when they do not sin, they make for themselves an image of Christ according to their own narrowness, reflect this falsified image, and mix up the various levels of depth within themselves; when we realize that only in the saint do we meet the true spirit of Christ and that only saints, as, for example, St. Paul, St. Augustine, St. Francis of Assisi, and St. Catherine of Siena, radiate an unfalsified image of Christ? Our gratitude should know no boundaries when we hear the priest pronounce, ''I will go in unto the altar of God (*Introibo ad altare Dei*)'' and the holy Sacrifice of the Mass begins; when ''O God come to my assistance (*Deus in adjutorium meum intende*)'' solemnly resounds at the beginning of the Divine Office; when we are enveloped in this ultimate, fully genuine world of truth; when we grasp that here, independently of our narrowness, errors and slumbers, God is adored in Truth and Spirit; that the true, genuine ''Word'' is spoken to God, because Christ Himself sacrifices, praises and glorifies God in our midst, and that *we* are allowed to sacrifice to God, to adore and praise Him through Christ, with Christ and in Christ. Then an endless stream of gratitude surges up within us. Then we experience what the Church is, what the Mystical Body of Christ is, and that God loved us first, before we loved Him.

It seems inconceivable, then, that so many Catholics feed on stones instead of bread, lead a life in which

their contact with this stream of divine life is so
limited, and so restricted to the mere duty of attend-
ing holy Mass on Sundays. Others, who attend Mass
more frequently and receive Communion, do not attain, in spite of this, a full conscious participation in
the mystery, because they only "pray in the Mass"
and do not follow the recommendation of Pope St.
Pius X to "pray the Mass." They do not know the Divine Office. Even among priests, who are *obliged* to
recite the Divine Office daily, there are some who do
this only as another duty. They are not aware that
through the Divine Office they are *allowed* to draw
from the true sources of the Spirit of Christ. Considering all this, we should like to shout to all those who
live in the House of God and who do not yet know
"the plenitude of the fruitfulness of the House of the
Lord (*ubertas domus Domini*)":

> O taste and see that the Lord is sweet!
> With joy shall ye draw water out of the wells
>   of the Savior
> And in that day ye shall say:
> Praise the Lord and call upon His name.*

---

* *Gustate et videte, quoniam suavis est Dominus.*
  Haurietis aquas in gaudio de fontibus salvatoris
  Et dicetis in die illa
  Confitemini Domino et invocate nomen ejus.

WORKS BY DIETRICH VON HILDEBRAND

In English

In Defense of Purity
Marriage: The Mystery of Faithful Love
Liturgy and Personality
Transformation in Christ
Fundamental Moral Attitudes
Ethics
The New Tower of Babel
Situation Ethics
Graven Images
What Is Philosophy?
Not as the World Gives
The Art of Living
Man and Woman
The Heart
The Trojan Horse in the City of God
The Devastated Vineyard
Celibacy and the Crisis of Faith
The Encyclical *Humanae Vitae*:
a Sign of Contradiction
Satan at Work

In German

Die Idee der sittlichen Handlung
Sittlichkeit und ethische Werterkenntnis
Metaphysik der Gemeinschaft
Das katholische Berufsethos
Engelbert Dollfuss: Ein katholischer Staatsmann
Zeitliches im Lichte des Ewigen
Der Sinn philosophischen Fragens und Erkennens
Die Menschheit am Scheideweg
Mozart, Beethoven, Schubert
Heiligkeit und Tüchtigkeit
Das Wesen der Liebe
Die Dankbarkeit
Ästhetik I & II
Moralia
Der Tod

BIOGRAPHICAL NOTE
Dietrich von Hildebrand
(1889-1977)

Hitler feared him and Pope Pius XII called him a "twentieth century Doctor of the Church." For more than six decades, Dietrich von Hildebrand—philosopher, spiritual writer, and anti-Nazi crusader—led philosophical, religious, and political groups, lectured throughout Europe and the Americas, and published more than 30 books and many more articles. His influence was widespread and endures to this day.

Although he was a deep and original thinker on subjects ranging across the spectrum of human interests, nonetheless, in his lectures and in his writings, von Hildebrand instinctively avoided extravagant speculations and convoluted theories. Instead, he sought to illuminate the nature and significance of seemingly

Liturgy and Personality

"everyday" elements of human existence that are easily misunderstood and too frequently taken for granted. Therefore, much of von Hildebrand's philosophy concerns the human person, the person's interior ethical and affective life, and the relations that should exist between the person and the world in which he finds himself.

Von Hildebrand's background made him uniquely qualified to examine these topics. He was born in beautiful Florence in 1889, the son of the renowned German sculptor, Adolf von Hildebrand. At the time, the Hildebrand home was a center of art and culture, visited by the greatest European artists and musicians of the day. Young Dietrich's early acquaintance with these vibrant, creative people intensified his natural zest for life.

In Florence, von Hildebrand was surrounded by beauty—the overwhelming natural beauty of the Florentine countryside and the rich beauty of the many art treasures that are Florence's Renaissance heritage. Pervading this Florentine atmosphere was Catholicism: in the art, in the architecture, and in the daily life of the people. These early years in Florence quickened in von Hildebrand a passionate love of truth, of goodness, of beauty, and of Christianity.

As he grew older, he developed a deep love for philosophy, studying under some of the greatest of the early twentieth century German philosophers, including Edmund Husserl, Max Scheler, and Adolf Reinach. Converting to Catholicism in 1914, von Hildebrand taught philosophy for years at the University of Munich.

However, soon after the end of World War I, Nazism began to threaten von Hildebrand's beloved southern Germany. With his characteristic clear-sightedness, von Hildebrand immediately discerned its intrinsic evil. From its earliest days, he vociferously denounced Naziism in articles and speeches throughout Germany and the rest of Europe. In response, the Nazis decided to kill him.

Von Hildebrand fled to neighboring Austria, where he continued teaching philosophy (now at the University of Vienna) and fought the Nazis with even greater vigor, founding and editing a prominent anti-Nazi newspaper, *Christliche Ständestaat.*

This angered both Heinrich Himmler and Adolf Hitler, who were determined to silence von Hildebrand once and for all and to close his anti-Nazi newspaper. Orders were given to have von Hildebrand killed in Austria. Although his friend and patron, Austrian Premier Engelbert Dollfuss, was murdered by the Nazis, von Hildebrand evaded their hit-squads and fled the country.

(It is characteristic of von Hildebrand that even while he was engaged in this life-and-death struggle against the Nazis, he maintained his deep spiritual life, and managed to write during this dangerous period his great spiritual classic, *Transformation in Christ.*)

Fleeing from Austria, von Hildebrand was pursued through many countries, ultimately arriving on the shores of America in 1940 by way of France, Switzerland, Portugal, and Brazil.

Liturgy and Personality

Penniless in New York after his heroic struggle against the Nazis, von Hildebrand was hired as professor of philosophy at Fordham University where he taught until his retirement. Many of his best works were written during this period and after his retirement. He died in 1977 in New Rochelle, New York.

Dietrich von Hildebrand was remarkable for his keen intellect, his profound originality, his prodigious output, his great personal courage, his deep spirituality, and his intense love of truth, goodness, and beauty. These rare qualities made Dietrich von Hildebrand one of the greatest philosophers and one of the greatest men of the twentieth century.

Sophia Institute

Sophia Institute is a non-profit institution that seeks:

— to restore philosophy to its true identity as a systematic inquiry into eternal truths about the nature of things;

— to clarify man's understanding of himself as a free creature capable of knowing objective truth through natural reason;

— to elucidate the phenomenon of objective values and their relation to human happiness; and,

— to demonstrate the central role that philosophy can play in resolving many of the crucial questions that confront man today.

Sophia Institute Press

Sophia Institute Press serves these ends in a number of ways. It publishes translations of foreign works to make them accessible for the first time to English-speaking readers. It brings back into print many books that have long been out-of-print. And it publishes important new books that fulfill the ideals of Sophia Institute.

Sophia Institute Press publishes books on philosophy as well as interdisciplinary works on topics in the humanities. These works revive and deepen many of the insights of traditional philosophy and integrate them with the legitimate advances of subsequent philosophies. The books published by Sophia Institute Press afford readers a rich source of the enduring wisdom of mankind.

Sophia Institute Press makes high-quality books available to the general public at modest prices by using advanced cost-effective technology and by soliciting donations to subsidize general publishing costs. In these ways, Sophia Institute Press ensures that its books receive much wider distribution than more expensive editions published by profit-making publishers.

A free descriptive catalogue of books already published will be sent to you on request.

Your Part

Your generosity can help Sophia Institute Press provide the public with inexpensive editions of works containing the enduring wisdom of the ages. Please send your tax-deductible contribution to Sophia Institute Press, Box 5284, Manchester, NH 03108. Your questions, comments, and suggestions are also welcome.

Sophia Institute Press is a tax-exempt institution as defined by the Internal Revenue Code, Section 501 (c) (3).